Leadership Gurus speak out!

Influence, innovation and performance in a changing workplace

Editors: Adele Alfano and Kathy Glover Scott ■

Published by
Experts Who Speak Books
www.expertswhospeakbooks.com

ISBN 978-0-9780283-3-6

Editors: Kathy Glover Scott and Adele Alfano
Book design and production: Creative Bound International Inc.
www.creativebound.com

Library and Archives Canada Cataloguing in Publication

Leadership gurus speak out! / edited by Adele Alfano and Kathy Glover Scott.

(Experts who speak series)
ISBN 978-0-9780283-3-6

1. Leadership   I. Alfano, Adele, 1959–   II. Scott, Kathy Glover, 1958–   III. Series.

HD57.7.L4264 2008   658.4'092   C2007-906990-8

Printed in Canada

Contents

Introduction

Throughout our six-year history as publishers of Experts Who Speak Books, *Leadership Gurus Speak Out!* is a title that kept arising in our planning sessions. As both of us are aware that when knowledge and timing come together, a powerful force is created (as with our publishing partnership), we parked this title, knowing that it would come to fruition in its own time. And here we are now!

Over the past six years, we've noticed a forceful shift in the field of leadership—and especially in leaders themselves. Leaders are going through a time of growth and change, often accompanied by growing pains. Tangible influences, such as changing business practices, tighter budgets and greater demand in not-for-profit organizations, instant access to information and immediate global communication and markets, directly impact how leaders lead. There are also more covert—or intangible—influences impacting leaders. People are quickly shifting their consciousness and thinking more about the value of their lives and their desire to take "their soul" to work. Though not as readily identifiable, people are bringing this into the workplace and asking those who lead them to respond.

Leaders need the new information and perspectives in this book. Speakers, trainers and coaches are also in great demand to assist with this area in the workplace. With all of the Experts Who Speak Books, our goal is to provide you with tips, tools, motivation and essential information. In *Leadership Gurus Speak Out!*, you'll find the collective wisdom, experience and knowledge of 13 top speakers, trainers, facilitators, coaches and consultants from across North America who specialize in leadership issues and innovation. Where else can you find the proven expertise and essential wisdom of 13 top trainers, coaches and consultants in one book? Each have taken the absolute essence of their work and teaching and condensed it into chapter form. And the information in each chapter is written with a focus on providing you with the new tools, skills and systems you need to excel, all in a format that is easy to read and reference.

What makes *Leadership Gurus Speak Out!* unique is how it speaks to the reader in a solution-focused way for leaders and those they lead in any size of business or organization. How roles that leaders have are rapidly changing and many of the old rules for leading (and being lead) are being challenged—or thrown out altogether. The diverse contributors and broad base of content in *Leadership Gurus Speak Out!* are indicative of the market for this multi-faceted information.

Experts Who Speak Books is one of the most successful book publishing companies in the world specializing in producing books for professional speakers, trainers, facilitators, coaches and consultants. We create co-authored books that showcase the dynamic, creative and successful people who have chosen these professions. We do it through supporting the writing process and taking care of all the specialized work of design, printing, publishing and distribution. And, we do it from a win-win value base, where cost sharing, cross-promotion and mutual support are the keys to our success. You are invited to visit our websites:

www.LeadershipGurusSpeakOut.com
www.ExpertsWhoSpeakBooks.com
www.AwakeningtheWorkplace.com
www.SalesGurusSpeakOut.com
www.ExpertWomenSpeakOut.com

Watch for our eleventh book, *Awakening the Workplace, Volume 3*, in 2008. Subjects for upcoming books in the series include the Internet, communications and marketing. Let us know if you are in these professions and would like to contribute.

All in all, you are holding in your hands a goldmine of information and expertise, geared to make your work life easier. Our wish is that success flows to you. The choice is yours—to remain where you are or move forward. Not a hard decision to make!

Kathy Glover Scott and Adele Alfano
Editors and Publishers, Experts Who Speak Books

Sid Ridgley MBA CSP

Simul Corporation

VIP Leadership:
The Three Things You Need to Master
to Create a Superb Legacy of Achievement

Maria and Mike are discussing the challenges and frustrations involved in pulling together the weekly inventory report. Jennifer, their manager, walks by, looks at them both and simply says "Are the two of you on break? Because I can find more work for you to do." In what should have been a reward moment, where two colleagues were working together to produce a better product, it became a negative moment where they were assumed to be goofing off and not working. In that moment, Jennifer had the choice to either lead or manage. *Managers control; leaders inspire.*

Once Jennifer is out of earshot, Maria says, "Think about it for a moment, Mike, boss spelt backwards is double S-O-B." Mike adds, "No wonder we have pitiful retention rates. No wonder we have poor loyalty. Who is there to be loyal to?"

Unfortunately, this scene gets played out far too often in far too many organizations. It is too easy to point a finger at Jennifer, the manager, and say that she simply doesn't know how to supervise; too easy to make excuses that in the three years since her appointment to the job she hasn't received any management training. In many organizations, the words "manager" and "leader" are used interchangeably when in fact they have different meanings. *Managers strengthen competence; leaders build confidence.*

Over the years of working with organizations that are underperforming, stress laden or resistant to change, we've learned that leaders are absent from the job. Sure, people still show up for work, but completing a task is not the same as making a contribution. To some degree, organizations have beaten leadership right out of their people in favor of creating a well-honed administrative and, quite literally, risk-adverse workforce. Many then wonder why the workplace feels demoralized, and lacks energy. Or why people are so disconnected. Or why people might be physically present, with their minds still at home.

Exercise: Why Should I Be Led by You?

Take a blank piece of paper and construct a 30- to 60-second commercial as to why you should be the leader. Just because you can do the jobs that you are supervising, or have been given the title "manager," simply doesn't translate into a solid rationale for you being the leader. This is not an easy task, though it is one that will provide you with increased insight into how to create a larger league of followers. Writing up your own answer to this question can help you become a better leader than you are right now. *Managers say "Go"; leaders say "Let's go."*

Before reading any further, take a minute and think of a person you have worked with who you believe is really an effective leader. I'm confident that when you do you'll conclude that all of the great people you worked with had something in common. They were passionate about getting the job done and equally passionate about growing their people.

After interviewing and working with literally thousands of managers and leaders, I have identified 15 skills or attributes associated with effectiveness in the workplace. As you read each, identify the attributes that, if worked on, would ensure that you are seen to be a better leader.

Attributes of Effective Leaders

1. **Firm grasp on reality:** They know exactly what's going on right now and have a realistic perspective.
2. **Altered behavior based on the situation:** An exceptional leader knows when a "kick in the pants" or a "quiet word" is the appropriate response.

3. **Belief that others' opinions are valid:** Searching for alternate opinions is important to a good leader as it leads to greater understanding.

4. **A moving forward mentality:** Being mired in the negativity of the situation is not where leaders will spend their time. Determining how to move forward and accomplish something is where the leader will invest their time, resources and talents.

5. **Learn from others:** Leaders don't expect to have all of the answers; however, they will search for sources from which answers can be obtained.

6. **Vision:** Though a somewhat overused word, good leaders have a sense of where they are going; they have a vision. They have an idea of what may be a worthy goal to achieve. Besides, if you don't know where you are going, why would anyone follow you?

7. **Being responsible:** Looking for others to blame is not a trait that is embraced by effective leaders. Holding people accountable is.

8. **Willing to teach:** Lessons learned by a leader are unselfishly shared with others, provided they are willing to listen.

9. **Good communicator:** A good leader stands out as a communicator in any group; they have honed their listening, speaking and presentation skills.

10. **Energy and passion:** Yes, they have both and they don't hold back on either.

11. **Trusting and trustworthy:** They know that in order to be trusted they must be first trustworthy. In order to get trust they must give trust.

12. **Resourceful:** Leaders know that they must be able to act effectively or imaginatively, especially in difficult situations.

13. **Consummate goal setter:** Successful people are great goal setters. They know that the process of setting goals immediately increases the likelihood of success.

14. **Focus on results:** Longer-term supervisors and managers know that it is really about getting results for their organization, whether they work in the for-profit or not-for-profit sector.

15. **Strong internal and external network:** Leaders know that their power often comes from, or at the very least is enhanced by, the sources of knowledge that they can access or acquire within a moment's notice. Successful

leaders work hard to ensure they have a strong network outside the organization and a very strong network inside the organization.

Years ago, I worked for a terrific leader who became my mentor and he helped me accomplish things that I know I simply would not have been able to had it not been for his influence. During one of my dialogue sessions with him—that's what he used to call them—he said, there are three types of people in this world: those who make things happen, those who watch things happen, and those who wonder what happened. He then asked me which type of person I wanted to be. What type of person do you want to be?

Of course I had made the decision that I wanted to be a "make it happen" type of individual. I knew deep down that unless I made things happen I would simply be an administrative person with a blown opportunity to tap my potential. He would remind me that employee surveys, over the past 15 to 20 years, have provided a consistent message: people working in organizations feel over-managed and under-led. Workers at all levels are looking for people that they can trust, who have passion, who have energy. He would inevitably go on to say that being successful in an organization, especially a larger organization, meant that you had to be a good manager *and* a good leader. It isn't a case of "either/or" but of "and/also." *Managers emphasize standards; leaders promote goal achievement.*

The Three Primary Functions of Being a Leader

In my work with numerous organizations throughout North America and India, I've learned that there is a cynicism among front-line workers as they look to the top of the organization. They see disconnects between the words printed on vision, mission and value statements and the behaviors that executives actually demonstrate.

Being successful requires us to be both a good manager and a good leader—focused on getting results and growing our people. People, for the most part, have an intense desire to belong, and want to make a contribution, to a vibrant organization that is relevant, sustainable and valuable to its stakeholders. In my view, it is the leader/manager who knows that the path to greater success rests with her/his ability to strengthen the following:

- **Customer value proposition**—the benefits, either real or imagined, that customers get when they do business with you and/or your company;
- **Employee value proposition**—the tangibles and intangibles that an employee receives from their employer in return for their performance on the job;
- **Shareholder value proposition**—the economic and/or sociological reasons why a person should become, or remain, an owner (by buying shares) of a company.

In order to achieve this, a leader needs to remember that he/she is a VIP (very important person), who is leading VIPs (employees), in their pursuit of professionally serving VIPs (customers).

The three primary functions of VIP leadership are: **value enhancer, independent thinker** and **people developer**. It's doubly critical for supervisors and managers to embrace the general spirit of the VIP philosophy while conducting the three primary functions. The reality is that these three primary functions are not independent; they are interdependent with one another. Having good people, who know what needs to be done and how to do it—who deliver on the promises made to customers, employees and shareholders—creates an achieving organization, focused on results. Let's examine each of the three functions:

#1—Value Enhancer

The very first function of a leader is to create value for the organization, value for the employees, value for the customers, and value for all stakeholders. As a value enhancer, the key to success is being able to see a future with possibility and, more importantly, being able to create or communicate a compelling picture of success. The value enhancer understands full well that the name of the game in corporate life, regardless of whether you're selling software, or cars, or insurance, or widgets, is that every business is in the same business: to get more customers, buying more, more often. The value enhancer working in government understands that it is about providing more quality service, to more people, more equitably.

Expectations on the Rise

In today's very demanding world of business, everyone is expecting more this year than they did last year. Customers expect more. Employees expect more. Owners/shareholders expect more. Though we may not be able to predict what customers and employees will want five years from now, what we can predict is that it will be more than what is provided today.

For Customers: The VIP leader remains close to the customers in order to understand what they truly value. They recognize that customer satisfaction, hence perception of increased value, is derived from the "intangibles" not the "tangibles" of the customer value proposition, for example, being treated with dignity and respect when doing business with the organization.

For Employees: The VIP leader also recognizes the fact that he or she is also part of the employee value proposition. It is true that employees want competitive pay and benefits, but it is also true that they want someone they can trust and believe in. They want someone to recognize and value the contributions that they make to the workplace. In fact, VIP leaders know that what employees want, *even more than money,* is recognition for having made a contribution to something that is meaningful.

For Owners and Other Stakeholders: The VIP leader works hard at fostering excellence in using organizational resources. They will utilize key measurements of performance to constantly and consistently make improvements to the organization's processes and activities. The VIP leader will help their people concentrate on the important activities, while removing those that are no longer meaningful or that get in the way of doing the job at the expected level of professionalism.

The leader who is a value enhancer recognizes that organizations, employees and customers expect to "get" value equal to or greater than what they "give" (in time, money, energy or loyalty).

From a people perspective, the value enhancer sees everyone as an important person in the organization. They encourage those they lead to be creative and innovative when soliciting input on work-related matters, and they will actively involve others when making important decisions about work.

From a task perspective, the value enhancer establishes clear directions and requirements for work-related activities. They have a good understanding of what it takes to get the job done and are focused on helping their followers get results from their work-related activities.

The value enhancer function of a leader helps her/him to set and achieve relevant goals, and to focus primarily on results, not process. In addition, they know how to link small activities to bigger goals so that people can actually see that they're making a meaningful contribution. The truth is, when we're seen as an individual who creates value in the organization, then the organization is more willing to continue to invest in us. Besides, what is the likelihood of continuing to receive a paycheck if we aren't providing something of value to our organization?

#2—Independent Thinker

Being the same as anyone else simply doesn't cut it anymore. Just because you may have the title "supervisor," "manager" or "director" does not automatically mean that people will follow you. They may have to because they're being paid to, but that doesn't mean that their hearts and minds are in it when they do follow. Successful leaders and managers that we've studied really exhibit an independent thinking quotient of unbelievable proportion because they will decide for themselves what is right and they will determine a direction in which they wish to go. Discovery consists of looking at the same thing as everyone else and thinking something different.

The VIP leader will have his or her own unique perspective of what needs to be done and why it needs to be done. Yet in every organization there is a popular, or what I like to call "herd," mentality towards just about every activity, function, process or product in the organization. Spouting what the herd is saying may be comforting because it is (after all) what everyone else is doing. But the independent-thinking leader has the confidence to consistently and constantly seek out opportunities for ongoing continuous improvement in everything they do. And they have the commitment to encourage and build this in others. Independent thinkers know that the disease is "status quo"; the cure is "change."

**The single most important trait of the independent thinker
is the ability to recognize that there are many right answers to
the problems that every organization faces. The independent thinker
will search for both the first and second-best "right" answers.**

The independent thinker has a lot of confidence and will actively seek feedback from customers or employees about how the organization performs its duties, sells its products, or looks after its customers. They also know that planning, and the need for creating a compelling picture of success from that plan, is hugely important for capturing the attention of those involved. From first-hand observation, it is clear that the independent thinker function is one that exists to simplify the complexities that people face in carrying out their jobs. When a manager simplifies and clarifies roles, responsibilities, goals and objectives, the likelihood of the person actually doing the job successfully increases dramatically.

From a people perspective, independent thinkers have the confidence to allow those they lead to follow through on ideas without always having to ask for approval. They will provide their followers with the authority to make decisions about their work, and they will provide opportunities for independent thought and action.

From a task perspective, independent thinkers seek to truly understand customer requirements, both internal and external. They will grant their employees sufficient power to satisfy customers. More importantly, the independent thinker will often be seen as a person who encourages and champions ongoing improvements to service levels.

The independent thinker is also an individual confident enough to go beyond brainstorming as a technique for generating alternate solutions to problems. As Albert Einstein once said, "Out of clutter, find simplicity. From discord, find harmony. In the middle of difficulty, lies opportunity."

#3—People Developer

At the end of the day, organizations do not achieve results—people do. The people developer function is one that strives to reduce ambiguity in order to establish clarity around responsibilities, processes, standards and, of course, outcomes. This function is about strengthening the competencies that exist in people while simultaneously building their confidence in doing the job. It is about fostering the independent professional accomplishment of goals and objectives. The VIP leader expects people to be professional in everything that they do and to be held accountable for the results.

The people developer function exists to ensure that people are engaged or connected to the work, its mission, its goals and objectives, its purpose and its standards. The VIP leader knows that there is a marked difference in performance between a person who shows up to do the job and a person who brings their heart and mind to the job.

The people developer sets and maintains high personal standards. One of the things managers who are people developers really know about and do exceedingly well is recognizing accomplishments. Whether this is just a simple thank you, or a gift, or the opportunity to attend a new training program, good people developers know how to recognize accomplishments—on both personal and team levels. They will promote collaboration and cooperation between individuals and departments. Most importantly, the people developer will help everyone extract the key "lessons learned" from both successes and failures. One of the principles by which a strong people developer operates is embodied in this statement: "You can tell people what they need to know very quickly, they will forget it just as fast. When you help people discover what they need to know, it remains theirs forever."

**The people developer has six key tools in their arsenal:
They can teach, tutor, counsel, confront, mentor and
coach (or some combination of these).**

More importantly, they work hard at building high levels of trust. The people developer knows that without a solid foundation of trust, the organization is bound for failure. After all, how long would you work for a person or an organization you didn't trust? Would you allow somebody you didn't trust to fix your car? Would you allow somebody you didn't trust to look after your child or your elderly parent? The truth is, you wouldn't.

The superb people developers I have worked with are a delight to watch. The manager who is a people developer knows and also understands that delegation, and especially empowerment, are the gifts of adulthood. This whole notion of empowerment is central to the development of people. Many managers don't understand the word "empowerment." They'll often think that it simply means letting people do whatever they want, and that's not true. Fundamentally, it means that the person is expected to act in a responsible manner in the best interests of the organization's customers and stakeholders. And they are accountable to do so.

People developers know the importance of promoting teamwork and cooperation in the organization. They also know that there is an overuse of the word "team." Calling a group of people a team simply doesn't make it so. Teams are created only through shared experiences: people learn together, play together, win together, lose together, or celebrate together.

From a people perspective, the leader who is a people developer encourages others to be open about their feelings and thoughts. They will encourage their followers to higher levels of proficiency by being an effective coach or mentor. But most importantly, they will recognize the performance of both individuals and teams.

From a task perspective, the leader who is a people developer will ensure that employees have the information, tools and training to do the job well. At the end of the day, the people developer function is focused on helping people be both professional and successful at everything they do. Without leadership, people will grow just enough to handle the problems that they face today; the challenge is to help them grow enough to expand their potential.

And, fundamentally, the most important thing I have learned working with literally hundreds of organizations and thousands of managers over the years is that people quit managers first before they quit organizations.

Exercise: Empowerment Assessment for Leaders

The following exercise will provide indicators of the people developer strengths that you (or the leader you are assessing) possess. The following can be used as a 360-degree assessment. If you choose to use it this way, you need to set up a process by which your raters can confidentially submit their information to an independent person for consolidation who will report back to you.

Leadership Gurus Speak Out!

By responding to the following statements in a candid and thoughtful way, you and the leader for whom you are providing feedback will gain a better understanding about what empowerment in the workplace means.

Please provide the name of the person you are rating: _____

The leader that I am rating:

	5	**4**	**3**	**2**	**1**
	Always	Usually	Sometimes	Rarely	Never
1. Encourages me to be open about my feelings and thoughts.	5	4	3	2	1
2. Establishes clear directions and requirements for work-related tasks.	5	4	3	2	1
3. Allows me to follow through on my ideas without first obtaining someone else's approval.	5	4	3	2	1
4. Ensures that I have the information I need to do my job well.	5	4	3	2	1
5. Sees me as an important person in this organization.	5	4	3	2	1
6. Seeks to truly understand customer requirements (internal/external).	5	4	3	2	1
7. Encourages me to higher levels of proficiency by being an effective coach.	5	4	3	2	1
8. Understands what it takes to get the job done.	5	4	3	2	1
9. Provides me with the authority to make decisions about my work.	5	4	3	2	1
10. Ensures that I have the tools to do my job well.	5	4	3	2	1

11. Encourages me to be creative and innovative when soliciting input on work-related matters.	5	4	3	2	1
12. Grants me sufficient power to satisfy my customers.	5	4	3	2	1
13. Recognizes my performance and appreciates my contributions.	5	4	3	2	1
14. Is focused on getting results from my work-related activities.	5	4	3	2	1
15. Provides me with the opportunity for independent thought and action on the job.	5	4	3	2	1
16. Ensures that I have the training to do my job well.	5	4	3	2	1
17. Involves me when making important decisions about work.	5	4	3	2	1
18. Encourages and champions ongoing improvements to our service levels to customers (internal and external).	5	4	3	2	1
19. OVERALL, I can grow and achieve results in this organization.	5	4	3	2	1
20. OVERALL, I value my working relationship with my leader.	5	4	3	2	1

Scoring:

Add all the numbers and divide by 20 for an overall score. Scores in the 4.4–5.0 range are excellent. Items rated 4.0–4.4 represent an opportunity to fine-tune your skills. Items rated 3.5–4.0 require improvement, and we would recommend having a discussion with those you lead. For scores less than 3.5, immediate attention is required, and we would highly recommend getting assistance from others in your organization.

The VIP Leader: Gaining Trust and Confidence

Every day you and I, as individuals and as managers, are faced with situations that test us as to whether or not we are trusting and trustworthy. We actually develop relationships based on the amount of trust that we hold for others. VIP leaders know that they cannot "technique themselves" to greatness—it starts with being trusting and trustworthy. Listed below are indicators that you've gained—or are in the process of gaining—the trust and confidence of others:

1. People are confident that you will live up to the commitments that you have made.
2. You have a reputation for keeping people in the know about things that affect them, always in a prudent, timely manner.
3. You respect confidences and refrain from disclosing what others have confidentially shared with you.
4. You tell it like it is, frankly and directly, when making progress reports or explaining how things are going.
5. You continue to support and implement decisions that have been informally agreed upon in conversations or impromptu meetings.
6. You consistently give credit where credit is due.

The VIP Leader: Demonstrating Loyalty and Responsibility

Just because the VIP leader understands the three primary functions of VIP leadership—value enhancer, independent thinker, people developer—does not mean that she or he will be successful. VIP leaders know that not only must they be good at these three functions, they must consistently and constantly demonstrate loyalty and responsibility to their organization and the people they lead. Here is what demonstrating loyalty and responsibility looks like:

1. You accept workloads without complaining to subordinates;
2. You express confidence in the top management of the organization;
3. You apply yourself and give yourself to the job;
4. You do whatever you can to help in an emergency or when severe problems arise;

5. You will go the extra mile to achieve goals that are meaningful to the organization and its customers;

6. You set an excellent personal example for others to follow;

7. You support proposals and plans that benefit the organization at large.

VIP Leadership in Action

All it really means when you've been appointed to the ranks of supervisor or manager, is that you're part of the management team—that part of the body of people who actually plan, organize, implement and control the activities and resources that go on within any organization. Your appointment to this rank does not guarantee that you're part of the leadership of an organization—though it's hard to believe that if you are a general manager you're not part of the leadership; of course you are. Being a general manager, however, doesn't guarantee that you are actually an effective leader. You and I also know that a person can be a significant "mover and shaker" within the leadership of an organization and not be part of the management ranks.

Whether supervising people directly or indirectly, the VIP leader knows that their current and future ability to "get things done" rests with their reputation as a value enhancer, independent thinker and people developer. It starts with being clear about the values you hold and the standards you expect. Employees like Mike and Maria are looking for those VIP leaders who know what it takes to create more value for customers, more value for the employees, more value for the stakeholders, and more value for the shareholders. Mike and Maria may never be the best employees, but they can "give" their best—something a VIP leader knows how to inspire them to do.

Sid Ridgley

Sid Ridgley, MBA, is an organizational development specialist who provides insights, guidance and practical tips for leaders in their pursuit of creating organizational workplaces that are customer and employee centered. He specializes in the areas of customer satisfaction and loyalty, sales, leadership development and front line-driven cultural change processes.

Clients that have benefited from Sid's expertise include: Siemens Canada, Hydro Ottawa, Horizon Utilities Inc., Zellers Inc., Holt Renfrew, Niagara Health System, Sutter Health, Catholic Healthcare West, Citigroup (India), American Express (India) and many others.

He is a co-author of *Transformational Leadership* (James & Brookfield Publishers, 2005) and the author of *Call Before You Dig! How electric utilities can connect with customers* (Simul Marketing Group Inc., 2005).

In addition to being an adjunct executive development professor for York University (Schulich School of Business), Sid is also a Certified Speaking Professional (CSP). He is the 2007 President of the Canadian Association of Professional Speakers, and his personal mission is "to help people focus their energy into growing their business and its people, and themselves."

Business Name:	Simul Corporation
Address:	65 Limeridge Street, Aurora, ON L4G 7X9
Telephone:	905-222-5534 or 888-291-7892 ext 29
Email:	sridgley@simulcorp.com
Web Address:	www.simulcorp.com
Professional Affiliations:	Canadian Association of Professional Speakers (National President 2007), International Federation for Professional Speakers, Canadian Society for Training and Development, American Society for Training and Development

A leader takes people where they want to go. A great leader takes people where they don't necessarily want to go, but ought to be.

Rosalynn Carter

Maureen Motter-Hodgson

Kairos Coaching Ltd.

The Top 10 Practices of Affirming Leadership

» Recently I had a disconcerting conversation with a friend who had suf-
fered a career-shifting and confidence-shaking year working under a very
toxic boss. She spoke of how her ideas were not listened to and how her
experience and skills were not valued. My friend left the organization and
it lost an incredibly talented and creative long-time employee who had
been a champion and an inspiration during her time there. «

This conversation is similar to others I've had over the years in my coaching and
consulting practice. I've observed too many people who have not felt valued in their
organizations, and have come to believe that the ability to affirm and value others
is a critical leadership skill that is directly related to the long-term sustainability of
organizations.

Toxic leadership is characterized by poor listening skills, autocratic behaviors and
ineffective relationships. These types of leaders can take highly creative, energetic
and talented employees and make them doubt themselves and their abilities. Just
as toxic chemicals erode and destroy their containers over time, toxic leaders can
erode their organizations.

People don't usually decide consciously to become ineffective or toxic in the
workplace. They are often unaware of the impact of their behavior and attitudes.
Unless their organizations have effective 360-degree feedback mechanisms—and a

surprising number of organizations today do not—or the leader has invited effective feedback through other means, a feedback vacuum can exist.

The old adage that people don't leave jobs and organizations, but rather leave poor managers or bosses, rings particularly true in today's fluid job market. People choose to leave corporations where their contributions are not valued. Marcus Buckingham and Curt Coffman, in their book *First Break All the Rules,* published an extensive study conducted by the Gallup organization that discussed this phenomenon, but recent research also confirms the trend. While toxic leaders can take competent, talented people and demoralize them, **affirming leaders** ultimately build confidence, competency and capacity in their people.

Fortunately, practices that lead to positive, affirming leadership can be learned and enhanced. I invite you to consider and explore the top 10 practices of an affirming leader.

Affirming Leaders: Top 10 Practices

#1—Impeccable Self-Awareness

A moment's insight is sometimes worth a life's experience.

Oliver Wendell Holmes

Self-awareness is defined as the ability to be a neutral observer of oneself and others and to gain awareness of our interactions with others. Self-awareness is critical to affirming leadership, because without it leaders tend to be on automatic pilot in their interactions and decision making. And self-awareness for leaders really serves two purposes:

1. It allows a leader to be more aware of him/herself and their impact on others "in the moment";
2. It allows the leader to be more aware of those around him/herself, and their impact on others over the long term.

Affirming and effective leaders take time to stop, step back, and observe themselves and others, and then step forward into action. Impeccably self-aware leaders know what can trigger moments when they are not at their best, or when they exhibit impatience, anger, defensiveness, uncertainty or lack of trust. From that awareness, a leader can choose a different way of interacting with colleagues, direct reports and clients.

Self-awareness provides leaders with the ability to readjust their behavior in the moment, as well as allowing them to be more mindful of what is being demonstrated by those they influence. Then, they are better able to intervene and assist direct reports, colleagues, and even their leaders, when they are not demonstrating impeccable self-awareness in their interactions with others.

So, how does one cultivate greater awareness? The first step is to slow down. In today's workplace, people often operate in default mode—moving in highly habitual ways, without consciously thinking of what they may be doing or saying. So much of life is spent moving at a frenetic pace that it is only when, and if, you press the pause button that you are able to be more aware of your external and internal life. Slowing down does not mean working less or becoming lazy; it means being more present and mindful in the moment.

Have you ever had the experience of driving home after work, parking your car, and then realizing that you remember little of the journey? All too often, that metaphor is an apt one for how we live our lives and how we lead in our organizations. Once you slow down and are in the moment, you begin to notice more. You start to notice more about yourself and more about other people. Slowing down, you can assess your physical, mental, emotional and spiritual state in that moment and how each of these may be impacting your interactions with others. Slowing down, you may notice that a colleague or team member is not their usual self and give them more direction, support, or even more space. Once you slow down and start to notice what is happening around you, you can reflect before acting, thereby making your actions more deliberate, effective, and purposeful.

An executive once told me that he had never really considered his impact as he walked out of his office or met people in the hallway and, as a consequence, felt that he had missed out on many opportunities to build better relationships with his colleagues and direct reports. Learning about intentionality had made him more committed to being so in his day-to-day interactions with his staff.

#2—One Hundred Percent Intentionality

In the long run, we shape our lives and we shape ourselves. And the choices we make are ultimately our responsibility.

Eleanor Roosevelt

Good leaders know their impact and great leaders are one hundred percent intentional about their impact. This ability to be cognizant and deliberate—to know and own your impact—is one of the key characteristics that differentiate toxic leaders from affirming ones.

» One of the most engaging demonstrations of the power of intent and impact was demonstrated at a conference I attended years ago in Atlanta, Georgia. The presenter asked everyone in the room to think of three words to describe her. While people were jotting down their adjectives, she wrote three adjectives on a flip chart that was concealed from the audience. Then she asked for people to call out responses to see how closely her adjectives matched those of the audience. While most of the adjectives that were offered did coincide with those she had written, one in particular did not. She had written "approachable" and several audience members indicated that she appeared quite intimidating. While her intent was clear, her impact did not match it, hence the lack of approachability that some people discerned. «

How often we sleepwalk through our days without considering the impact of our leadership presence. Asking ourselves the classic coaching question, "How do I want to show up in this moment?" can provide a great structure for becoming more intentional in our dealings with others.

Know, too, that while acting with intent can strengthen our impact, this is not a strategy to be used manipulatively. We must strive to be consistently genuine and sincere in our intent.

**The greatest payoff in becoming more intentional at work
and in daily life is that the closer your intent matches your impact,
the greater the trust that is engendered in relationships.**

Here is a methodology to build greater intentionality, especially in the role of leader:

- Identify five trusted colleagues you believe will be frank and honest with you. (For those who are truly courageous, include some direct reports and your boss.)
- Now, ask them to provide you with three adjectives to describe you. In advance, reflect upon and write down three adjectives to describe the impact you want to have when interacting with these people.
- Compare their lists with your list of adjectives and discuss similarities and dissimilarities.

#3—Silence the Inner Critic

You must act as if it is impossible to fail.

Ashanti Proverb

Everyone has an inner critic—that voice inside your head that uses fear to keep you from moving forward, taking risks, or living life fully. It goes by many names—the skeptic, the saboteur, the impostor, the censor, or the irritating roommate. Regardless of what it is called, affirming leaders learn strategies to silence it, or push it aside, while they choose to take action.

In his book *Taming Your Gremlin*, Richard Carson discusses a number of ideas and strategies to reduce the impact of the negative inner critic. The first, not surprisingly, is awareness. Until you can be aware of what your inner critic tells you—and be able to refute it—you cannot still its chatter and move forward. Not giving in to the inner critic, and instead relying on your inner ally to help you to grow, develop and make choices, allows you to move more purposefully through your work and life. Once you become adept at silencing or stilling your negative self-talk, you can assist others to identify and silence their own. Being an ally for others around their own inner critics allows you to champion them and help them build their own strengths and capacities.

Silencing your negative self-talk is a life skill that can serve you well. Strong leaders learn to silence their inner critic even when it is at its most active. Affirming leaders help others to identify and learn strategies around silencing their inner critics.

This exercise can be used with colleagues or subordinates to help them identify their inner critics:

- Ask them to think of something courageous, or perhaps even outrageous that they'd really like to do in their work or life.
- Educate them about inner critics and ask them to listen for any internal voices that may be telling them why they'd not be successful or why they "shouldn't" be thinking of doing this.
- Have them articulate verbatim what their inner self-talk is about the topic while you listen closely for any messages that are not accurate, are fear-based, or are overly critical.
- As an external ally, help them to find sufficient data to refute this inner critic by reflecting back to them where you hear their inner critic's message as inaccurate.
- Encourage them to ignore the inner critic's voice and take one step toward realizing their goal. Action begets further action and is a powerful antidote to the inner critic's chatter.

#4—Leverage Your Signature Strengths

Leadership is an art, a performing art. And in the art of leadership, the artist's instrument is the self.

James Kouzes and Barry Posner,
The Leadership Challenge

Years ago there was a movement around performance management that focused on eradicating a person's deficits, or at least closing the gaps. We've learned that a more progressive and energizing way to address this is to actually look for the signature strengths that people possess—those qualities that make them unforgettable as leaders and employees—and leverage these.

So, what are those "signature strengths" that you bring to your role as leader? Is it your ability to communicate with clarity, or your skills to inspire and motivate others? Or perhaps it is your capacity to be decisive in implementation, or to see the bigger picture. What other "quiet strengths" do you possess as a leader? Is it your compassion, humility or humor? Regardless of your strengths, it is important to be mindful of how you utilize and build upon them. While this does not preclude knowing which of your skills need further development, it means that you will focus more on maximizing your strengths while finding ways to compensate for the areas that may be challenging for you.

#5—The Art of Sincere Acknowledgment

The deepest principle of human nature is the craving to be appreciated.

William James

People often equate acknowledgment with praise and recognition. And yet, acknowledgment is quite different. While praise and recognition imply kudos for what you have done, acknowledgment, in its truest form, is about *who* you are, not *what* you are doing. This is the difference between being told "great job on that presentation" versus "I'd like to acknowledge your commitment to communicating with heart."

>> Early on in my leadership journey, I had the privilege of working with one of the most affirming and effective leaders of my career. She was then Dean at a major post-secondary institution and one of her practices involved handwriting personal notes to each one of her staff when they had reached a notable milestone or gone the extra mile. She would thank people individually for their contribution and, in doing so, spoke

to who the person was, not simply what they did. Her signature strength was her enormous capacity to affirm and develop others, to see their inner being and take the time to acknowledge them. It was not surprising that those around her felt that their talents were valued, and her staff was fiercely loyal to her. **«**

We don't always know the impact of our words; what we can be sure of is that the positive ones can make a profound difference in people's lives, just as negative words can be devastating.

#6—Demonstrate Conviction

> *A moment of choice is a moment of truth. It's the*
> *testing point of our character and competence.*
>
> Stephen Covey, *Principle-Centered Leadership*

Another characteristic of affirming and effective leadership is conviction, which is the ability to know what to do and to act resolutely. Conviction flows from your core values. Ineffective people are often seen to act from little conviction, being buffeted at every turn by the opinions and judgment of others. They do not stand firmly in their position. The leader with conviction acts without hesitation when a challenging decision is required. And they do this while keeping open to the perspectives and ideas of others.

Aligning your core values with your work and life allows you to be more confident in your conviction to act. And while there is no surfeit of discussion these days about values in organizations, there often is a real absence of owning what these values really are, in identifying gaps, and in identifying how close the alignment is between the person and the corporation. And with the latter, when the alignment is missing, people leave organizations. Having a method or strategy to identify these core values and see how they align is critical. This provides the foundation to lead with conviction. Here's one way to think about your core values in your role as leader:

- What is the leadership legacy you'd like to be known for in your organization?

- What five leadership values are most important to you as you consider this legacy? (Examples might be: passion for excellence, integrity, authenticity, or relationship building.)
- On a scale of one to ten, how well are you currently honoring these values in your work and life?
- What one action might you take immediately to have greater alignment between your values and your desired legacy?

#7—Courageous Authenticity

The privilege of a lifetime is being who you are.

Joseph Campbell,

The Hero With a Thousand Faces

The ability to act and live authentically is our seventh crucial point for affirming and impactful leadership. Courageous authenticity for a leader is fuelled by living from convictions. While there has been much talk of the importance of authenticity in leadership—especially over the last decade—there is also still great hesitation in being "really real." Many leaders feel that they must fit some company model of leadership and that being just who they are is not enough.

It is frustrating and lonely when a person feels they cannot let their true self come to work and instead feel a great need to conform. Affirming and effective leaders are able to be themselves and be vulnerable enough to let others see who they are; these leaders give those around them full permission to act authentically too.

Courageous, authentic leaders will be clear on their core values and act in alignment with them in spite of the repercussions. Courageous authenticity is often integrity in action, and it is not always about taking enormous risks. The definition of courage may differ from person to person, and the actions that make for courageous action may also differ. So, what does courageous authenticity mean to you? If you had all the courage and authenticity in the world, what would you do? What's standing in your way?

#8—Engage in Difficult Conversations

> *Our work, our relationships and our lives succeed or fail*
> *one conversation at a time.*
>
> Susan Scott, *Fierce Conversations*

One of the more common challenges today for people in organizations is in having difficult conversations with others in the workplace. Affirming and effective leaders have the courage to engage in honest dialogue with the people they lead. This means not only naming "the elephant" when it is in the room, but also means having other difficult conversations as they arise in the workplace.

The hallmark of a great leader is his or her capacity to communicate courageously while remaining aware and intentional about their impact. And allowing others to provide feedback in the moment about the conversation sets great leaders apart from mediocre ones.

Preparation breeds confidence when engaging in challenging conversations. The following exercise may be helpful as you prepare for some of the difficult conversations you need to have in your work and life:

- Reflect upon a courageous conversation you need to have (it may be with a colleague, a direct report, or *your* leader);
- Be intentional about how you want to show up in the conversation (e.g. open, non-defensive, confident);
- Now, envision the desired outcome from the conversation;
- Ask yourself the following five questions:
    1. What additional information do I require in order to have this conversation?
    2. What assumptions might I be making that may be erroneous?
    3. How will I demonstrate being receptive to the other person's ideas during the conversation?
    4. What are the benefits of having this conversation?
    5. What is the cost of not having it?

#9—Develop Relationships to Engender Trust

In organizations, real power and energy is generated through relationships. The patterns of relationships and the capacities to form them are more important than tasks, functions, roles, and positions.

Margaret Wheatley,
Leadership and the New Science

No longer seen as a soft skill but rather as a key performance competency in many organizations, the capacity to build strong relationships is critical for leaders in the corporations of the future. James Kouzes and Barry Posner speak of a study done by the Center for Creative Leadership in their book *Encouraging the Heart*. The CCL found that "relationships with subordinates" ranks as the number one success factor when studying the top three jobs in organizations, and that the factor that significantly differentiated highest performing managers from the lowest performing managers was their score on "affection"—the degree to which they showed warmth and caring to their employees.

In addition, a colleague recently shared with me that his organization was now addressing succession planning and leadership development by assessing the relationship-building capacity of its employees. While technical proficiency was once the yardstick to gauge the effectiveness of leaders in the workplace, the litmus test is changing.

The bedrock of great relationships is trust, a place from which all conversations are possible. While trust can be a nebulous concept, we all know when we trust someone and when we don't. The ability of a leader to engender trust, through having impeccable self-awareness and awareness of the impact they have on others, can allow them to have different relationships with those they lead. Those leaders who are skillful at building and sustaining positive relationships with people around them will be the ones who will survive and thrive in the changing workplaces of the future.

#10—Build Capacity in Others

The way you see people is the way you treat them, and
the way you treat them is what they become.

Goethe

The ability to build capacity in those around you is something that sets great leaders apart. Just as a plant grows toward sunlight, people gravitate to those who see the best in them, and help them to develop and leverage their strengths. An affirming leader is one who sees possibility and potential in others and then helps them to develop their abilities. Building capacity and capability in others through mentoring or coaching is seen as a performance measurement for today's leaders. It is also a key performance skill in today's workplaces. People want to be around those who see their potential and will take the time to help them develop their strengths.

Benjamin Zander is the conductor of the Boston Philharmonic Orchestra and co-author of *The Art of Possibility*. He is so incredibly passionate about leadership development that his enthusiasm is contagious. Benjamin is a diminutive person, yet his presence is huge as he speaks about leadership. Zander teaches the powerful concept of holding people as "A"s; that instead of grading people as a "B" or a "C+", we can actually start to hold everyone in our work and life as an "A."

Upon returning from a conference after hearing Mr. Zander, I was sharing his message with a colleague who exclaimed, "But not everyone *is* an 'A.'" I realized that he'd missed the point—that our having the capacity to see someone as an "A" even when they may not be acting that way is an incredibly powerful concept. People know when we're grading and assessing them, and they know when we can see their potential and are sincere about helping them to achieve it. Seeing the potential in others and being committed to bringing it out is one of the greatest gifts a leader can give to others. Our ability to see the true potential and essence of others allows us to nurture our own potential and brilliance too.

Developing an appreciative eye for the capacity of others means looking for their strengths—those things that make them uniquely who they are—and helping them to leverage their abilities. Leaders who have the capacity to develop and hone their appreciative eye are given the opportunity to lead from a new place of commitment, energy and enthusiasm.

Here is a reflective exercise to help build capacity:

1. Think of a member of your current team or a specific direct report. Identify what unique strengths he or she contributes to your organization;

2. Consider strategies to assist in developing and leveraging these strengths further;

3. Commit to sitting down with this person and offering assistance to help him or her develop further.

Activating Affirming Leadership Practices

New models of leadership must prevail in order for organizations to survive and thrive in this millennium. The intergenerational workplace, combined with a projected skills shortage unprecedented in the last century, will require men and women to demonstrate affirming capabilities in order to motivate and retain others.

Through enhancing self-awareness, intentionality, silencing the inner critic, leveraging your signature strengths, sincere acknowledgment, demonstrating conviction, being courageously authentic, engaging in difficult conversations, developing relationships, and building capacity in others, you will have the opportunity to leave a legacy of affirmation and validation.

As Marcel Proust so eloquently stated, "The only real voyage of discovery consists not in seeking new landscapes but in having new eyes." With new eyes, we can build more affirming workplaces and build greater capacity in the people who inhabit them.

Maureen Motter-Hodgson

Maureen Motter-Hodgson is principal of Kairos Coaching Ltd. As an energetic and inspiring coach, facilitator, speaker and educator, she has assisted hundreds of individuals, teams and organizations to identify their signature strengths and to develop their leadership capacity and presence.

Maureen designs and delivers customized learning programs and presentations for corporations that want to maximize their learning advantage in today's competitive workplace. Working with leaders, Maureen challenges them to more authentically express their affirmative leadership style, and to build stronger relationships with others.

She brings to her clients 25 years of rich and diverse experience focused on workplace learning. Maureen's directness, compassion and enthusiasm are hallmarks of her approach to her work and she believes that cultivating affirming learning cultures from within not only provides highly sustainable results for organizations and teams, but can permanently transform relationships. Maureen believes that "great leaders build capacity in their people utilizing an affirming and appreciative approach" and that ability will be the key to creating highly sustainable workplaces in the future.

Maureen has a Master's Degree in Education (specializing in Adult and Community Education), the Coaches Training Institute (CPCC) coaching certification, and training in Appreciative Inquiry in Taos, New Mexico (with the methodology's founder). She has experience also as a teacher and facilitator for the University of Calgary in Alberta.

Business Name: Kairos Coaching Ltd.
Address: 11 Strathcanna Court S.W. Calgary, AB T3H 1Z1
Telephone: 403-217-0564
Email: kairoscoaching @shaw.ca
Web Address: www.kairoscoaching.com
Professional Affiliations: Calgary Association of Professional Coaches (past
                        President), International Coach Federation

Favorite Quote:
Leadership and learning are indispensable to each other.

John F. Kennedy

Rolande Kirouac

Spadrole

Leading With Laughter!

*S*top, don't make me laugh, my teeth will go flying! My mom used to be self-conscious about her dentures. However her flying teeth have been a source of laughter for the whole family. In my mind's eye, I see all of us sitting at the kitchen table; something funny is happening and everyone is laughing. Suddenly my mom's teeth go flying. There is a slight moment of panic, we all wait for it, and then my mother bursts out too. We are rolling with laughter!

My mom is the "laughter leader" in our family. Her connection with us through healthy laughter taught us all about the positive energy that can be created through laughter. These are such great memories and such a wonderful legacy. Merci Maman!

Leading With Laughter! is a unique approach to organizational wellness that needs to be implemented by everyone, and everywhere—including schools, businesses, clinics and hospitals!

Laughter is not only good medicine, it's good business.

Develop healthy laughter and be the leader you are meant to be! Build balance and better relationships, and increase productivity and confidence simply by using laughter skills spontaneously and strategically in the workplace. Mirth, laughter, celebration, festivity, hilarity and joking—in the proper context and setting—are great catalysts for creating positive work environments.

Reasons We Stop Laughing

We lose permission to laugh as we get older, and past beliefs tell us not to be silly, or rather to get serious. We have been told to "grow up" and have fallen prey to the belief that in order to be taken seriously, everyone should be serious! In 1983, Josef Scheppach stated in an article that, despite huge rises in our standard of living, we only laugh six minutes a day, and 40 years ago it was 18 minutes. At international congresses dealing with therapeutic humor in Switzerland and Germany, Drs. William Fry and Patch Adams have said that children laugh 400 times a day and adults only 17 times.

Children laugh all the time. They can be playing very seriously and one of them will just laugh. The laugh will come from way down in the belly. For children, laughter is very natural and free flowing. The following are four key reasons why we adults laugh less—especially in the workplace:

#1—We Fear Looking Bad

As adults our laughter is often not free flowing. We hold it back, suppress it or change it, making sure that it's a *good* laugh: not too loud and not too long, avoiding all inclinations of spitting, coughing, snorting and other unmentionables. As well, the laugh has to be appropriate and at the right time. If the boss is telling a joke, we have to make sure to laugh at the appropriate time and for the same amount of time as our co-workers. We are also afraid of wasting time, being talked about, laughed at, not taken seriously, losing our teeth, and looking silly.

Everyone wants to look their best. When we are laughing, we are sometimes afraid that the people around us might find us silly or ridiculous. The truth is that we are not going to be looking our best as we are bent over and roaring with laughter. Laughter is about letting go, letting it rip, and just going with the moment. As we start laughing, the mind will say: *Stop it, I think I look stupid.* We have to learn to ignore the mind and answer back with *So what!* Furthermore, everyone around us who is joining in the laughter is actually not looking their best either. Take a bit of time to reflect on this: why would anyone judge laughter as being ridiculous?

#2—We Forget How Good It Feels

We lose touch with our own sense of feeling good. We become consumed by the needs of our children, co-workers, parents, projects, mortgage payments and retirement funds. Our sense of success is measured in monetary and status values.

The benefits of smiling, giggling or laughing include reduced levels of stress hormones (epinephrine and cortisol), and increased levels of endorphins (the body's natural painkiller), which leads to better sleep, improves lung capacity and oxygen levels in the blood, and helps control high blood pressure—plus it just feels GOOD!

Feeling good must be THE measurement of success for healthy leaders. Leaders who feel good can do a lot of good in this world. Leaders who don't feel good, become dysfunctional.

#3—We Disconnect From Our Smile Sources

A few years ago, I realized that I had become a dysfunctional leader. Life was not fun or funny anymore. I realized that I needed to reconnect to activities and things that generated a smile for me. They worked when I was a younger, so I figured why wouldn't they still work today?

Do you remember what tingled your senses as a child? Take a few minutes to relive these moments. What were the sounds, smells, movements, touches, tastes and sights that generated a smile for you then? As a child, my body, mind and spirit came alive through the sounds of birds, the smell of sweet clover, playing baseball, eating fresh bread, and looking at sunsets. These are some of my smile sources.

Start by making a list of the sources that create a smile for you. If your list is not very long, don't worry; this is where begging, borrowing and stealing come in. Talk to your family members, partner, friends or co-workers about your smile sources and ask them what puts a smile on their faces. In doing so, the energy created will not only change your world, it will change the whole world around you. This will increase your smile sources. I know it sounds crazy, but it works!

#4—We Fear Being Inappropriate

Studies have found that dominant individuals do use humor more than their subordinates. If you've often thought that everyone in the office laughs when the boss laughs, you're very perceptive. Philosopher John Morreall says that controlling the laughter of a group—hence the emotional climate—becomes a way of exercising power. However, when laughter is generated with sexist, racist, sarcastic or ironic comments, you can be sure that someone out there is not laughing! The long-term side effects of toxic humor are devastating: it destroys morale and creates cliques; the workplace becomes blasé, and eventually laughter diminishes all together.

When we assume leadership positions, we sometimes bring with us a tendency to use toxic humor. It has more power than a bag of peanuts in a zoo! Many leaders walk away from humor and laughter, fearing that they might use toxic humor. Don't do it! Laughter must be sustained and nurtured, not suppressed. Leaders need to take a bold stand and create healthy laughter for themselves and the people around them.

**We need to discover how much delight we live in
and how we can offer this to others.**

The Benefits of Laughter in the Workplace

We are born with a built-in energy source, but as adults we sometimes lose it. Laughter brings it back; it is the child within. Feel as wild and free as a child. Laughter is free from attachment to worldly aspirations. It is dynamic and empowering.

Scientific research shows that smiles and laughter, even if artificially induced, actually stimulate pleasure centers in the brain. French neurologist Dr. Guillaume Duchenne mapped 100 facial muscles and discovered that those false or even half-hearted smiles involved only muscles of the mouth. But "the sweet emotions of the soul," he said, activate the *pars lateralis* muscles around the eyes. He discovered that when lips part and turn up, the eyes crinkle and show crow's feet, and the upper lip droops slightly, then there is heightened activity in the left anterior cortex of the brain, which is the center for happy emotions.

Exercise

Try this now (and later at work). Make a fake smile and then stretch it out until you move the muscles around the eyes. Hold it for 15 seconds. Make note of how you feel. When you try it at work, how do you feel? How does it improve your energy level?

Laughter in the workplace is being rediscovered as an innovative way to fight stress, improve morale, and increase camaraderie and motivation. Laughter Yoga is a systemic program designed to easily reintegrate this ability we all have. A Laughter Yoga session is an experience that will introduce you to a most refreshing and innovative approach to stress management. Daily 20-minute laughter sessions lead to scientifically measured stress reductions of 50 percent or more.

» Dr. Madan Kataria, a family physician from Mumbai, India, was very impressed by American journalist Norman Cousens' book *Anatomy of an Illness* and the research work undertaken by Dr. Berk from Loma Linda University. Dr Kataria found that the human mind doesn't know how to make a distinction between fake and genuine laughter. Either way it produces happy chemistry. His wife, Madhuri Kataria, brought in her experience as a yoga teacher and suggested gentle breathing and other yoga exercises be included in the routine to deepen its impact.

Together they created Laughter Yoga—a blend of yogic deep breathing, stretching, stimulated laughter exercises, and cultivated childlike playfulness. This technique generates laughter for no reason. Started with just five people in 1995, it has grown into a worldwide movement with more than 5,000 clubs. «

A Mini-Vacation at Work

As my body started practicing laughter on a regular basis, my mind became a lot more focused on positive energy. It is now much easier for me to promote and create positive energy. I was able to get a better perspective on myself and my life. I took on scuba diving, kayaking, a new relationship, and started my own company with vigor and confidence, knowing that anything I wanted to do was attainable. What a great feeling! My spirit woke up. I felt connected to my gut feelings, my sense of intuition and, best of all, my wisdom.

Leading With Laughter! works well because it's clean, safe and neutral. It pushes away the world and its problems, providing the most wonderful mini-vacation. The problems do come back; the difference is that we are now empowered to handle them. The more you do it, the easier and better it is. Laugh till it hurts. Laugh often, long and loud.

Here is another way that laughter rescues our health: According to Dr. William Fry of Stanford University, laughing two hundred times burns off the same amount of calories as ten minutes on the rowing machine. A study by the University of Maryland Medical Center found that people with a well-developed sense of humor were less prone to cardiac problems.

Appropriate Emotional Expression at Work

Difficult times can manifest themselves in so many ways. These are the times in our lives when there is loss, pain, confrontation and frustration. Learning to express the emotions of life in a healthy manner is the first step to feeling better. Sometimes there are tears. Afterwards, we have to let go of the fears and sorrows and get back to the laughter.

Knowing when and how to get back to the smiles and laughter can be difficult. Don't be afraid; laughter will come to the rescue. One of my clients told me a story that made her realize that turning a difficult environment into a positive one is easier that we think. Her story is called "Music for the Soul":

» Lynne is a nursing supervisor on the night shift in a hospital in Western Canada. One night as she is finishing her reports and looking forward to getting home and having a good sleep, Mr. K, usually a quiet and very gentle patient, is ringing his bell again. When Lynne enters his room, all Mr. K wants is to have his pillows fluffed.

She's a little frustrated; not only has she been running around all night with other patients but she does not know how to help Mr. K get to sleep. She fluffs his pillows and tucks him in, knowing very well that he will be ringing again in ten minutes. On her way out of the room something triggers in her; Lynne turns around and decides to stay and chat for a bit.

They talk about music, accordion players from different parts of the world, and especially about a classic song by Edith Piaf, "La vie en rose." They both agree that it's a wonderful song. Lynne tucks Mr. K in again, says goodnight, and goes back to work.

On her way home, as Lynne passes by Mr. K's room, she hears an accordion. She goes into his room and finds him sitting on a chair with his accordion playing "La vie en rose." Mr. K looks up and smiles.

Lynne is completely taken in; she stops, takes a deep breath, and spends a few minutes listening to the sweet sounds of the accordion. Later she reflected on how she had stopped to create a new environment and had a smile put on her weary face. She realized that talking about something that had nothing to do with being in the hospital or being a patient was the wisest thing she could have done, for both herself and for Mr. K. **«**

**When two people share a smile
it is the closest thing to a miracle!**

What Leaders Need to Know

Moving a troubled and sensitive situation towards laughter is high risk. Remember the flying teeth? My mother knows that this can either be very humiliating or very funny. Maman chose to laugh at her own flying teeth, giving us permission to laugh along! The following are three tips that will help you bring more laughter to your workplace:

1. Identify and avoid toxic humor: We know that the temptation of dipping into the bag of peanuts and pulling out toxic humor; we ALL resort to toxic humor at one point or another. "Humor is a tool like any other," says Robert L. Weiss, a psychologist at the University of Oregon who studies humor in relationships. "People use humor in lots of different ways, including some negative ones. Almost every sweet, supportive way of using it has an evil twin: an aggressive, selfish or manipulative version. And like those teasing comments in the workplace that can just as easily feel like flattery or an attack, the two sides of humor are so intimately intertwined, it almost isn't funny."

The following story demonstrates how a leader's misuse of laughter turns toxic:

» Derrick is the marketing director for a big company in Toronto. He has been with the company for three months and is adapting well to all the different tasks and responsibilities he has within the company. He likes the company and wants to succeed.

A staff meeting has been called. Derrick walks into the boardroom and sees an empty chair beside Susan. Susan, the head of the Human Resources Department, invites him over. Mr. Harris, the company CEO walks in; he is looking worried. Everyone is anxiously awaiting his announcement.

Mr. Harris hands out the annual report with next year's projections. It has been a difficult year so changes have to be implemented in order to adjust. Mr. Harris blames no one, but jokingly adds that if the company had a better Human Resources Department things might be different. Everyone laughs, except for Susan. After all, it is a funny comment and it did relieve some of the tension.

When the meeting is adjourned, Derrick turns to Susan; she is upset. Susan is wondering why she is the butt of Mr. Harris' joke. Derrick understands her frustration and makes his excuses for laughing along at Mr. Harris' joke. Derrick is wondering how he can change this environment. «

Often, the person in a group who takes a stand is not necessarily in a leadership position; they are, however, demonstrating good leadership skills. It is the actions we take, not our job titles, that make us leaders. Derrick did the right thing in recognizing Susan's feelings. Should Derrick talk to Mr. Harris about his use of toxic humor? Will Mr. Harris listen and accept his comments?

People in official leadership positions must be prepared to be challenged and accept constructive comments from their co-workers in order to change a toxic environment into a positive work environment. Using the energy of our co-workers to promote healthy laughter and build positive work environments is crucial.

2. Learn to deal with difficult people: Creating a positive work environment can be challenging when we are surrounded by difficult people. Most traditional work environments thrive on competition and uniformity, thus creating suspicion, aggressiveness, and resistance to change. When implementing change in our workplaces, dealing with difficult people is part of the challenge.

When I make presentations, clients ask me what I think can be done with people who do not want to laugh. The agonizing grouches, the persistent pessimists, the eternal criers will not go away; given all the time in the world they will not change. These difficult people choose to spend most of their time living in this state. Our choice is whether or not we accept this state of mind in our own lives.

Laughter is contagious. So are negative states of mind. Both will impact the overall energy of the group. Do not confuse difficult people with people who are actually going through difficult times. People dealing with difficulties must be given time and space to do so. This does not make them difficult people. It is important to know the difference and we must intervene only in the case of difficult people.

Trying to change the state of mind of difficult people can be a total waste of energy. We have to accept that another person's state of mind is not our responsibility. The fact remains, people change because they want to change. However, remember that working on maintaining our own positive state of mind will inspire others to do the same. Staying focused on feeling good is a good example to set and will help some difficult people to seek and maintain a positive state of mind.

Everyone must be committed to the process of creating and nurturing positive work environments in order to achieve any results. Difficult people need to know that they are not to interfere with the energy of the group. Clear boundaries need to be set. Sometimes we need to intervene, to take a stand, and set the boundaries. Criticism, complaining, and doomsday predictions must be checked at the door; only constructive ideas and solutions can move the organization forward. People who are not committed to this process must be asked if they want to stay or leave. This question must be addressed.

3. Laugh from the top down: Learning to smile, giggle and laugh has huge implications. Take it seriously; make a commitment to take the necessary steps toward building more laughter into your life and work environment. **Leading With Laughter!** is a concept that needs to move from an idea to a core value for ourselves and for our workplaces.

You are the captain of your ship; only you can make this commitment and set the course for smooth waters, gentle breezes and blue skies. You have to eat, you have to sleep, and you have to deal with everyday life. Why not do it with a smile, a giggle, and a laugh? Your body, emotions, mind and spirit need regular nourishment, so refill with energy and start feeling good for a change! You have to feel good to do good! As a leader, you may need to take some bold steps to increase laughter in your own life in order to facilitate change and instill laughter as a way of life in your work environment. Get to know your staff, peers and colleagues. Observe what makes them tick and, more importantly, what makes them laugh!

Laughter is the sun that drives winter from the human face.

Victor Hugo

What is it that puts a smile on your face? How are you going to get the smiles going for everyone around you? This will help build balance and better relationships. It will help you retain your employees and it will also attract potential new ones.

Laughter is not only good medicine, it is good business. Integrating **Leading With Laughter!** into your workplace will help you and your co-workers to develop healthy laughter skills. Everyone will invest in creating positive energy. Find a systemic way—such as starting a Laughter Yoga club—in your workplace.

Great leaders desire to leave their mark—a legacy—in the workplace and on the people that they serve. How about being the leader who was not afraid to laugh?

Rolande Kirouac

Rolande Kirouac delivers a refreshing and innovative approach to organizational wellness. She believes that leaders who can learn to smile, giggle and laugh more easily and more often, foster cooperation, creative thinking, job satisfaction and a workplace where employees want to be. And her programs and presentations teach them how.

A certified Laughter Yoga teacher, Rolande has trained dozens of leaders to promote the health benefits of "laughing for no reason." Over 1,000 people have received the health benefits of her program. Owner of the Winnipeg-based consulting company Spadrole and co-creator of the laughter CD *HA!*, Rolande builds on her extensive experience in stress management, leadership development and team building to help organizations become more effective and efficient.

Rolande has taught clients from such diverse backgrounds as health care, education, justice and administration how to access their inexhaustible power source of laughter and build healthy work environments. Rolande has logged over 10,870 laughter hours and has appeared on national and local television and in the print media.

Business Name: Spadrole
Address: 440, De La Morénie Street, Winnipeg, MB R2H 2Z3
Telephone: 204-256-6215
Email: info@spadrole.ca
Web Address: www.spadrole.ca
Speaking Affiliations: Canadian Association of Professional Speakers, Professional Member, Winnipeg Chapter

Laughter is not only good medicine, it's good business.

A leader's role is to raise people's aspirations for what they can become and to release their energies so they will try to get there.

David Gergen

Cara MacMillan

BMO Nesbitt Burns

The Power of a Leader

> *Our deepest fear is not that we are inadequate. Our deepest fear is that we are powerful beyond measure. It is our light, not our darkness that most frightens us. We ask ourselves, Who am I to be brilliant, gorgeous, talented, fabulous? Actually, who are you not to be? You are a child of God. Your playing small does not serve the world. There is nothing enlightened about shrinking so that other people won't feel insecure around you. We are all meant to shine, as children do. We were born to make manifest the glory of God that is within us. It's not just in some of us; it's in everyone. And as we let our own light shine, we unconsciously give other people permission to do the same. As we are liberated from our own fear, our presence automatically liberates others.*
>
> Marianne Williamson

Leadership is a choice and a responsibility. So often we choose to play small. Because it is safe. When we choose to transcend our present situation and live with joy, we risk offending people who are afraid. They, too, had a choice to transcend their situation but chose the status quo. One of my heroes is Viktor Frankl. In his work *Man's Search for Meaning*, Frankl wrote that the freedom of choice is the gift of being able to choose our own attitude. We cannot control the actions or situations of our lives, but we can choose to control our reaction to them. Frankl also observed that the meaning of life is not as complex as we choose to believe. We find the meaning of life in each and every moment that we choose to live in balance. Whether we are prisoners of the Holocaust, as Frankl was, or prisoners of the fears in our own minds, our ability to transcend and change is directly proportional to the depth of our spirituality. Now, I didn't say religion, I said spirituality. Some of us express it through religion, others express it through meditation, but the common denominator is hope. Our ability to accept and integrate change as individuals is directly proportional to our faith in the future. When one loses faith, one lives in chaos.

Frankl made another key observation: there are only two races of humans, decent and indecent. No society is free from either of them. We each can choose our race as well; we each choose to be decent or not. Yet so many times we see decent people who choose to live in fear. The choice to live in such chaos means that they will also be a member of the indecent race. Fear leads to apathy. Apathy leads to inaction. When individuals no longer care, they have lost their faith in the future. This leads to the power of the ego. We all know people whose obsession with control gives them a false sense of security. Pity them. They live in fear and chaos. In this chapter, we will be reviewing the lives of three people who chose to be great. They chose to control their reactions to negative situations and to transcend their fear. They chose to be great.

Today we are in a time of climate crisis. Climate change is the greatest challenge our globe has faced since the Cold War and the arms race. And those who are leading the transition to a newer economic model are those who understand true power. Power is not ego; it is the ability to connect with an energy source that transcends ego. There have been few true leaders in our times, yet we can each name them. They are the individuals who did not steal energy or creativity from their teams; they are individuals who inspired action. Leaders give energy so that a team may overcome inertia and move forward. In this chapter, we will be evaluating the process of leading change. We will have a look at how key leaders in climate change, including Dr. David Suzuki, Dr. Gro Harlem Brundtland and Al Gore, are successfully leading our planet to change. From their examples, you'll glean insights to increase your leadership compassion with a larger vision and greater focus.

Leaders who inspire teams to change and grow have first followed their own path to change. The steps have different names, depending on which evaluator you choose to follow, but what I put forth is a model from Earl Nightingale. The first step of leading change is simply to accept the change as reality. In this step, individuals stop worrying or fearing a situation and sit down and assess it rationally. The second step is to do a risk assessment of the change. My figure skating coach used to say, "What's the best that can happen? What's the worst that can happen?" If you can live with either, then what is the risk? This is interesting. Many of us get stuck in this phase. Not because we fear the worst outcome, but because we cannot visualize a positive outcome. Leaders can visualize both. The third step is to assess how to mitigate the worst and the best scenarios. What are all the options? Leaders create plans to facilitate change and to control the variables that can be controlled. The fourth and final step in change is to implement and monitor the results. You will often find that the change is a healthy and positive step. There is a sense of relief and vitality as one moves from chaos towards control. Chaos is a state of mind that is filled with fear. Control is a state of mind that is balanced and grounded. Leaders of positive change transition quickly through this process. Their ability to inspire comes from a grounded and balanced state of mind.

Qualities for Change Leadership

Climate change calls for a different type of leader than what we are accustomed to. We are not talking about leaders like Winston Churchill or John F. Kennedy who rallied people against a common foe. In climate change, a leader needs to inspire individuals to change. This is **community leadership**. There are two principles of community leadership: the first principle is that community leadership is about relationships. For example, strong community leaders understand group dynamics, are team players, inspire others to change, and share responsibility, thus empowering the group. They share power.

The second principle of community leadership is that it is about change. Community leaders focus the energy of the group on change and/or improvement.

The leadership qualities of a community leader are consistent. The first is that they are self-aware. They have taken the time to understand themselves, their beliefs, strengths, weaknesses and behaviors. These leaders are authentic. They have empathy for others. They are competent in their abilities and their skills. One of the critical qualities of a community leader is the power of their commitment. Their actions speak louder than their words.

The qualities of the groups that they lead are also consistent. On their teams, one will find collaboration. The group works well together, each member bringing his or her own strengths to a task such that they create a synergistic outcome. In other words, the sum of the parts is less than the whole. The team has a shared purpose that each member can easily articulate and understand. There is a division of labor. Each member pulls his or her own weight. There is disagreement, but it is conducted with respect and unity. And ultimately, the most important and most enjoyable aspect of teams that are led by a community leader is that a learning environment is created where each individual is encouraged to grow.

Community leaders have common skills. The first is self-esteem. The second is strong communication skills. They speak well, listen well, and are excellent observers. They have outstanding teamwork skills. And finally they have excellent conflict resolution skills; they can handle conflict with creativity, respect and non-violence.

The most critical success factor of each community leader is how they use their power. Let's define power as the ability to shape our world. Each of us has access to our own personal power. Some of us are more aware of this ability than others. As Viktor Frankl says, we each have the power to choose. When we choose to be a leader, we choose to use our power. A dictator wields power over others, puts them down using coercion, violence and force. A leader lifts people up with their collaborative power, supporting and nurturing others.

Definitions of leadership are all well and good, but without concrete examples it is difficult to understand how to apply the concepts. In the next section, we will look at three community leaders who are having success in empowering their immediate teams and others they spur into action. The first leader is Canadian David Suzuki, CC, OBC, PhD, a prominent scientist, broadcaster and environmental activist. The second is Dr. Gro Harlem Brundtland, the former Prime Minister of Norway, a diplomat, physician and international leader in sustainable development and public health. The third and final example is Al Gore Jr., the 45th Vice-President of the United States, businessman and environmentalist. Each of these individuals is an expert in his or her field and in the practice of true community leadership.

Dr. David Suzuki

Dr. David Suzuki is a third generation Japanese-Canadian. His family was a victim of the Canadian government's decision to intern people of Japanese origin during the Second World War. Although this completely uprooted his family, including the forced sale of the family dry cleaning business, a young David followed the lead of his father and tried to make the best of a horrific situation. This was the time in his life that his passion for nature was sparked. As he refers to this experience, "This was biology as it should be learned, firsthand in the wild, joyously and effortlessly."

Suzuki's career led him to many other places as well, and in each of his new environments, he looked for an opportunity to learn something new about nature, a new species, fish, insect, amphibian, bird or mammal. This period of his development taught Suzuki a critical leadership skill: change management. He practiced the ability to accept change as reality and find the positive in each new challenge.

His love for nature evolved to a passion to protect it when Suzuki returned to British Columbia with his children. He took them to a favorite fishing place of his youth and they found themselves in an ancient forest, as he describes in *The David Suzuki Reader*, published by Greystone books in 2004:

> *This was a forest shaped by the forces of nature for ten thousand years, a community of life where death gave birth to new life in an endless recycling of nutrients through countless species that make up a forest. We had stepped into it from the edge of industrial logging, which would soon transform it into something infinitely simplified and unrecognizable. In those few minutes that my children and I had entered into the forest temple, I had recognized the terrible hubris of the human economy. To transform this matrix of life-forms, soil, water, and air into a war zone where soil, air, water, and life were so degraded was a travesty of stewardship and responsibility to future generations.*

It was at this epiphany in his life that Suzuki accepted a calling to become a community leader and focus on change and improvement. He focused his work and his family on environmental activism.

Another characteristic of a community leader is self-esteem. Suzuki lacked this characteristic until later in life. His internment during the Second World War left psychological scars and feelings of inferiority. His self-esteem blossomed when he witnessed the economic disaster of B.C. logging. Suzuki found his voice. He began to speak with confidence and passion about nature preservation, and in so doing launched his career in broadcasting.

A third quality of a community leader is excellent relationship skills. Suzuki speaks of his parents' accomplishments through the war as truly remarkable and more amazing than anything he has ever accomplished. Nominated as one of the top ten "Greatest Canadians," Suzuki publicly stated that his vote was for Tommy Douglas, Canada's premier social democratic leader, who was the eventual winner. Suzuki practices what he preaches. In 2007, he traveled across the country in a diesel tour bus to share the message of climate change. Carbon offsets were purchased to compensate for tour activities. Suzuki spread his message and left a zero footprint on our environment.

David Suzuki first brought his message of environmental activism to children with two programs: *Suzuki on Science* and *Quirks and Quarks*. He later introduced a successful adult program, *Science Magazine*. Since 1979, Suzuki has hosted *The Nature of Things*, a CBC television series that has aired in over fifty countries. Through these programs, Suzuki has been able to bring his message of nature preservation, threats to our ecosystem, alternatives for sustainable living, and alternative energies to a wide audience.

Today, Suzuki is the spokesperson for alternative energy and energy conservation. The campaign "You have the power" encourages each individual to make conservation choices where they can.

Dr. David Suzuki is an excellent example of an influential Canadian community leader. Through the many changes of his youth and his career, Suzuki became adept at dealing with change on a personal level. He searches for the positive in each environment and situation. Suzuki has built strong alliances as he collaboratively works with business, media and education to spread his message of nature preservation. He is humble. He practices what he preaches. Most importantly, he uses his power to empower others to treat our environment with respect.

Dr. Gro Harlem Brundtland

Like David Suzuki, Gro Harlem Brundtland had a childhood that was filled with change. She moved with her parents from Norway to the United States and then to Egypt, finally returning to Norway. Her father was her role model, teaching her to practice what she preaches and to make a difference in this world. He encouraged her to develop her own ideas and to express them. His faith in his daughter gave her a strong sense of self.

Brundtland is a medical doctor who entered politics at the early age of seven. Her father was also a medical doctor who specialized in rehabilitation medicine. He was a prominent member of Norway's Labour Party, a United Nations expert, and a family man. Her family life was clearly formative, as Nancy Gibb's article, "Norway's Radical Daughter" (*Time*, 25 September 1989) revealed:

> At dinner time, she often questioned her father about the political issues he faced in cabinet. "I was always asking, 'Why are things so? Why can't we do more?'" In addition, Brundtland's parents encouraged their daughter to believe that women can achieve the same things in the world as men.

Brundtland began her political career in earnest in the seventies. She lobbied for women's rights and subsequently was elected to parliament in Norway. In her first executive position, she served as Minister of the Environment. Later she would become the first woman Prime Minister, Chair of the World Commission on Environment and Development, Director-General of the World Health Organization, and a member of the Panel of Eminent Persons on the United Nations Conference on Trade and Development, as well as U.N. Special Envoy for Climate Change. As she explains about her career:

> There is a very close connection between being a doctor and a politician. The doctor tries to prevent illness, then tries to treat it if it comes. It's exactly the same as what you try to do as a politician, but with regard to society.

Gro Harlem Brundtland's most significant contribution came as Chair of the World Commission on Environment and Development, which today is widely referred to as the Brundtland Commission. The political concept of sustainable development was developed and introduced by this commission. This work became the foundation and momentum for the Earth Summit. The political concept that Brundtland authored, published in *Our Common Future*, the Report of the World Commission on Sustainable Development, is this:

> *Sustainability is development that meets the needs of the present without compromising the ability of future generations to meet their own needs.*

Brundtland has very strong communication skills. Recently she spoke at the Canadian Conference for Responsible Investing. Gro speaks with sincerity and an infectious common sense that inspires her audience to commit to action to combat climate change. She is a respected international leader who continues to look for ways to improve our world in the areas of health and the environment. On July 18, 2007, in Johannesburg, South Africa, Nelson Mandela, Graça Machel and Desmond Tutu convened a group of world leaders—known as The Elders—to contribute their wisdom, independent leadership and integrity to tackle some of the world's toughest problems. Gro Harlem Brundtland is a founding member of The Elders. This is her ultimate recognition as a community leader. Brundtland is recognized as a global leader whose power comes from within and is shared without. Nelson Mandela has been quoted as saying that The Elders are the true community leaders of our globe. "This group can speak freely and boldly, working both publicly and behind the scenes on whatever actions need to be taken," he commented. "Together we will work to support courage where there is fear, foster agreement where there is conflict, and inspire hope where there is despair."

Albert Arnold "Al" Gore Jr.

Gore's father was the U.S. Representative and later the Senator for Tennessee. Al grew up living in a hotel in Washington D.C. during the school year and then returning to the family's working farm each summer. During this time of nature and space, he nurtured a love of the outdoors:

> ...the farm was a different kind of experience. I couldn't wait to get back there; I loved the farm. As a kid, I often walked with my father over every part of the place, learning from him to appreciate the details of the terrain. My dad taught me the moral necessity of caring for the land.

Gore attended Harvard College during the 1960s. It was at this time that he experienced his first epiphany. In his natural science class, he met his mentor, Professor Roger Revelle, the first scientist to propose measuring the impact of carbon dioxide on the earth's atmosphere. Revelle shared his research with the class, illustrating that the overwhelming amount of carbon dioxide that is being dumped into our atmosphere is affecting the temperature of our earth. Revelle was able to project into the future the potential impacts of global warming. There is one variable that Revelle underestimated. It was the timeline. Global warming occurred at a faster rate than was ever anticipated.

Al Gore left Harvard College in his last year to pursue a seat in Congress. He was successful and naively set off to spread the word about the environment. Gore brought his mentor to congressional meetings, but all the lobbying fell on deaf ears. Although still dedicated to nature, other political issues also came to the forefront. The second epiphany occurred when Gore was critically injured in a car accident. Through this period of healing for the Gore family, each member was given the gift to focus on what is truly important. As Gore relates:

> I truly believe that I was handed not just a second chance, but an obligation to pay attention to what matters and to do my part to protect and safeguard it, and to do whatever I can at this moment of danger to try to make sure that what is most precious about God's beautiful Earth—its livability for us, our children, future generations—doesn't slip from our hands.

Al Gore Jr. has very strong communication skills. The best example of this is his work *An Inconvenient Truth*. Gore combined an award-winning book, movie and presentation into a powerful call to action that has become the tipping point for climate change. In working with influential scientists, media experts and his family, Gore found a medium that presented his passion and message to a world in a way that could be heard and understood. And now he is a Nobel Peace Prize recipient for these efforts.

Al Gore Jr. had the opportunity to take his controversial presidential defeat and turn it into a bestselling non-fiction drama. Instead, he took this adversity and turned it into an opportunity to make a stand on climate change. His ability to rise above defeat and disappointment is the ultimate example of a community leader. He chooses to take the road less traveled and in so doing inspires many. As he observes:

> *An astonishing number of people go straight from denial to despair, without pausing on the intermediate step of saying, "We can do something about this!" And we can.*

The Community Leader in You

Let's summarize what we have talked about with respect to community leadership. Community leaders engage with the flow of energy. Their power comes from within and transcends their egos. Each has a higher purpose, a reason for working to improve our world and make a difference—and is a visionary in making it happen. They have exemplary change management skills. They accept change readily, do risk assessment, and are able to visualize both positive and negative outcomes. They plan and implement their reaction to change, and monitor the results.

Climate change calls for superb community leadership skills. This involves collaboration, communication, and the ability to inspire others to act. Dr. David Suzuki, Dr. Gro Harlem Brundtland and Al Gore Jr. are all examples of excellent community leadership. As individuals they each practice the ability to shape their own worlds and the future of our combined world. With humility and perseverance, they have overcome hardship, change and, in some cases, persecution to protect our living world. Their message is presented in a manner than can be heard and acted upon by others. They have given us an example, but it is up to each of us to follow our own path to community leadership. As inspired by them, the following are ten things you can do on *your* path to community leadership:

1. Be authentic;
2. Engage with the flow of energy;
3. Be an advocate for hope;
4. See only two races of humanity: decent and indecent;
5. Let your actions speak louder than your words;
6. Ennoble and empower your teams;
7. Lift up others...don't drag them down;
8. Believe that you can shape your world;
9. Encourage others to grow;
10. Be humble.

Cara MacMillan

Cara MacMillan is an investment advisor with BMO Nesbitt Burns. Cara entered the investment industry in 2003, building on her previous executive experience in strategic management, customer service and professional services within the high-tech sector. Cara holds an MBA from Athabasca University.

She is married to David, and together they are blessed with a son and a daughter. Cara and David are very involved in their children's competitive sports.

Cara believes passionately in education. She continually contributes articles to both national and community magazines. She teaches investment seminars. Cara is currently writing an investment book for children.

Company Name: BMO Nesbitt Burns
Address: 1600 Carling Avenue, Suite 700, Ottawa, ON K1Z 1B4
Telephone: 613-798-4237
Email: cara.macmillan@nbpcd.com
Web Address: www.caramacmillan.com

Charles Seems

HR Spectrum

Making Powerful Presentations:
A Holistic Approach for Leaders

A good leader is one who communicates well. Communicating to groups requires effort and practice. Many great ideas and concepts have not succeeded because they weren't properly communicated. Don't let that happen to you! Getting your message across effectively to your audience may mean the difference between success and failure. As Dale Carnegie pointed out in 1921, "Great speakers are not born, they're trained."

Great leaders communicate regularly. While some leaders are effective public speakers, many need to brush up on their skills before setting foot on the platform. Although public speaking is one of the many skills you require to be a great leader, it is *the* skill that can make a huge difference in your career. Think back to how often in the last year or two you have been asked to make a presentation. Were you satisfied with your presentation? Was the feedback positive? What could you have done to improve your performance?

Is This Speaking Engagement Right for Me?

Public speaking is the hardest form of storytelling. To reach such a lofty goal, you must become a *raconteur par excellence*. People will come to hear you, but unless you truly entertain them, they will "tune you out." The expression "talking heads" is descriptive of those presenters for whom the audience is not important. What's a presenter without an audience? An expensive resource wasting everyone's time!

Some of the ideas in this chapter are not new, but taken together they may provide you with startling results. Never underestimate the power you hold when making a presentation. Entrance your audience and you'll have them eating out of your hand. Ignore the time-tested ideas in this chapter and you'll find yourself speaking to an empty room.

While you may be able to refuse speaking engagements that are offered to you, there will be occasions where you will be called upon to make presentations. A polished delivery from an engaging speaker will bring about benefits long after he or she has left the platform. Recall those excellent teachers and professors from your past and try to identify what made them so memorable. In order of importance, list the skills you believe are paramount to an effective presentation. Your list may look like the following:

- Speaks in a variety of tones;
- Engages audience with real-life stories;
- Uses humor effectively;
- Respects everyone in the audience;
- Speaks clearly in order to be heard;
- Knows the subject matter well;
- Takes questions from the audiences without getting ruffled;
- Uses (automated) tools to enhance delivery.

Making each presentation the best it can be requires that you set aside some time to plan what you will say and how you will deliver your message. Without effective public speaking skills, a leader will miss out on opportunities to make a difference. Good leaders are able to rally the troops and get people moving, not so much by what they say but rather by how they say it.

As a leader in your field, you'll want to make sure that, where possible, you are accepting those speaking engagements that will further your ideas and concepts and thus improve your career prospects. Before we get into the details of what makes a memorable presentation, the first question should always be: *Is this speaking engagement right for me?*

To help you decide whether or not you should accept a speaking engagement, consider the following exercise. Based on your results, you should have some indication as to whether or not you should seriously consider the offer. In the following chart, respond with a "Yes" or "No" to each consideration for accepting a public speaking engagement.

Considerations for accepting a public speaking engagement	Yes 10 points	No 5 points
The subject matter is of great interest to you.	_____	_____
You know the subject matter very well.	_____	_____
You have presented on this topic before.	_____	_____
You have successfully worked with this client before.	_____	_____
You have adequate time to prepare the presentation.	_____	_____
Your presentation has great appeal to most audiences.	_____	_____
If travel is involved, you will have time to get acclimatized before you begin the presentation.	_____	_____
You have back-ups in case things go wrong.	_____	_____
You feel great when you are presenting.	_____	_____
You are open to suggestions for change to the content of your presentation.	_____	_____
Totals	_____	_____

Now, tally your score. If your total is 60 or less, you may wish to reconsider the offer. If you accept the offer to speak, it's time to start getting ready.

Back to Basics

So you think your presentations are great?
Are you really sure? What makes a memorable presentation?

It takes nerves to get up and speak; however, there are tips and tricks of the trade that can be very helpful. As practice makes perfect, so will you improve with time and experience. You may be shaky (literally) when you first start making presentations, but as you gain the confidence that comes with practice, your delivery will improve and your nerves will settle down.

Public speaking starts in school with "show and tell." Teachers know that public speaking is an important skill, and perhaps this is why they have insisted over the years that each student be able to stand up in front of peers to show and describe something. I'm sure you've been subjected to "show and tell" and that you probably hated standing up in front of your classmates. There was always that nagging feeling that peers would think that your topic was not very "cool" or, worse, that you were absolutely boring. The whole experience could be nerve-racking, particularly if you were unprepared. Imagine (or remember) forgetting your "show and tell" object and having to find a replacement when you were already at school!

Although there are things that cannot be controlled in public speaking, most fall under the category of items that can be planned for or anticipated. This chapter is divided into two parts. In the first part, we'll focus on the presenter, and in the second part, on the presentation.

Part I: The Presenter

My clothes are pressed, my hair is combed,
I have a copy of my speaking notes; therefore, I'm ready!

My approach to effective presentations takes into account all aspects of the person presenting, as well as the material being presented and the audience to whom the presentation is being made. This holistic approach serves to ensure that the best possible outcome will be achieved as all aspects of a successful speaking engagement have been thought through and acted upon.

Not so fast! Although all of the above is important, it is but the tip of the iceberg. There are many aspects to getting yourself ready for a presentation. Simply showing up groomed and dressed appropriately will not suffice. Remember that the audience has come to the presentation to hear a performer. Performers use an elevated platform to demonstrate their skills, thus the expression "platform skills."

Platform skills can be learned by doing (trial and error) or by reading books on this topic.[1] Leaders with superb presentations skills are seldom born that way. And although the gift of storytelling is extremely useful, it takes more than that to make powerful presentations. But I'm getting ahead of myself; more on that in the second part of this chapter.

Through years of personal experience, it has become clear that success in public speaking engagements rests on being both physically and emotionally prepared to face an audience. Most audiences are unforgiving, and you will lose them physically or intellectually if you're not at your best. Being at your best will require that you arrive prepared. How does one prepare?

Imagine, for a moment, a presenter who seems well prepared but doesn't notice that the audience does not understand what is being presented. Imagine a presenter who looks tired and yawns. Regardless of the expertise of the presenter, nothing can compensate for lack of attention to detail or lack of attention to the audience.

Whether the presentation lasts for 45 minutes or is given over two days, the same level of performance is expected. It is difficult to reach high levels of performance without being in the best possible physical condition. Top leaders and public speakers know the importance of maintaining a healthy lifestyle in order to offer peak performance each and every time they are on the platform.

A healthy lifestyle requires that you maintain good nutritional habits, exercise daily, rest/sleep adequately, and refrain from excesses that could hinder your performance. It is a delicate balancing act. To be able to harmonize all your daily activities and remain healthy and in control requires consistent effort.

Diet

Diet is one of your best allies. Good nutrition ensures that your body can function properly and will help in providing the stamina you'll need to stand for hours, even days, before a group of people. Proper nutrition helps with memory and reduces the

---

1. Books to consider include *101 Leadership Actions for Effective Presentations* by Ollie Malone, 2004; Renaissance 5005: *Making the Most of Presentations (Leadership Toolkit: Communications and Meeting Skills for Leaders)* by Bob Applegate, Patricia Reuss, Joyce Hart and Anna Geist, 2005; *The Art of Public Speaking* by Stephan Lucas, 2007.

chances of indigestion—and halitosis. (This may not be an issue when you are speaking, but it can certainly have a negative impact when you meet with participants before or after the presentation.) The following are three diet directives:

1. A well-balanced diet includes food from all four food groups. Canada's Food Guide helps unravel the mysteries of healthy eating. For more information, you may wish to access their website at www.healthcanada.gc.ca/foodguide.

2. Nutritional information is also available from the famed Mayo Clinic in Rochester, Minnesota, which has released its top 10 list of healthy foods. Here, in alphabetical order, are the Mayo's picks: apples, almonds, broccoli, blueberries, red beans, salmon, spinach, sweet potatoes, vegetable juice, and wheat germ. For more information, you may wish to access their website at www.mayoclinic.com/health/health-foods/NU00632.

3. The following are known dietary irritants and you should attempt to reduce or eliminate them from your diet: red meat, refined white flour, refined sugar, salt, yeast, caffeine, and saturated fats. Together or in combination, these make you either sluggish or hyper.

Although you certainly do not want to be hungry while standing up and making a presentation, you should avoid ingesting large quantities of food just before stepping up on the platform. Allow yourself time to digest food before your presentation. My research indicates that most presenters allow 30 to 60 minutes of rest after eating and before going to the platform.

Essential Self-Care Tips for Powerful Speaking

Exercise: We know that exercise is essential to overall health and energy levels, and it is even more critical for a speaker. Include stretching and cardiovascular exercises in a 30- to 40-minute daily program.

Rest: Power naps of no more than 20 minutes are really effective to get your energy back up to level. Tune out outside noise and concentrate on relaxing every part of your body and you will feel rejuvenated even if you haven't fallen asleep.

Sleep: Most people need seven to eight hours of sleep each night. Public speaking requires your complete attention so that you can pick up on cues and clues. Adequate sleep will serve you well.

Self-hypnosis: By instructing your subconscious on modifications you wish to make and behavior patterns you would like to change, through positive constructive suggestions, you can bring about beneficial changes to your well-being. If self-hypnosis is new to you, try self-hypnosis tapes, which are available at your local library or bookstore.

Part II: The Presentation

Powerful Presentations

Having taken care of your physical self, you can now turn your attention to the mechanics of preparing your presentation. As a leader, the knowledge you have of the topics you will speak on should be sufficient for you to know how to organize the material you want to share with participants. In this second part of this chapter, the focus is on the "how to." Know that not all presentations will require the level of skill suggested by the tips included in this section.

50 Professional Tips for Powerful Speaking

The following tips have helped even the most experienced leaders to make powerful and memorable presentations. The tips are listed in no special order but are grouped under common headings. Reading these tips every once in a while will remind you of important points that you may have overlooked in your most recent presentations. Bookmark this list so that you can easily access it.

Audience
1. How many people will be attending your presentation?
2. What type of work do they perform?
3. What do they know about the subject matter you are presenting?
4. What are the goals of the attendees?

Objectives of the Presentation
5. Are you informing, persuading, selling, or any combination thereof?

6. Identify the salient points you want your audience to remember and weave them into your presentation.

Anticipate Attendees' Questions

7. Know the points on which your audience is likely to want more information.
8. Know the points on which your audience will likely challenge you.
9. Plan how you will mitigate any negative comments made during or after the presentation.

Volume, Pace and Pauses

10. Ensure than you can be heard at the back of the room.
11. Draw people in by slightly lowering your voice and raise it to put emphasis on important points or to bring to their attention specific information.
12. Speak slower when making an important point.
13. Speed up when the information is easy to understand or less important.
14. Use 5- to 10-second pauses in appropriate places while speaking, just as you would use punctuation in written language. This will give you time to give your vocal chords a rest. For participants, it gives them time to think about what you just said.
15. Use pauses to collect and organize your thoughts.
16. Use a relaxed but serious tone.
17. Use humor with great care; avoid jokes that might offend anyone.
18. Avoid filler words or expressions: "You know," "As I was saying," "Maybe it's just me but...," "Like," "Awesome." Record your presentation, listen for these annoying filler words/expressions and try to eliminate them.
19. Move around the podium and, if possible, walk towards the attendees.
20. Use facial expressions as appropriate to express surprise, concern, empathy and understanding.
21. Smile naturally.
22. Use eye contact to make participants feel included and to show your interest in them.
23. Limit eye contact to 3 to 5 seconds; otherwise, you may make someone feel uncomfortable.
24. Check to see if your attendees are still interested. If eye contact diminishes, it's a sign they are losing interest.

25. Gesture naturally; if presenting in a foreign country, find out about offensive hand gestures to avoid.

Getting a Grip on Nerves

26. Accept the fact that you will have a certain degree of nervousness that will dissipate once you proceed with your presentation.
27. A certain degree of nervousness can be a positive thing in that it can boost your energy level, thus making it easier to achieve an enthusiastic delivery.
28. Knowing your material well will reduce your overall nervous tension.
29. Look for trust and acceptance from the audience to reduce your nervousness.
30. Keep in mind that audience members will see you as qualified to deliver the material you are presenting.
31. Use examples that are relevant to the audience.
32. Get to know a few people before your presentation starts to get a sense of familiarity and to determine their concerns.
33. Look for these people in the audience occasionally for reassurance.

Standing at the Podium

34. Dress appropriately for the audience.
35. Wear comfortable clothing.
36. Avoid loud and aggressive colors and/or patterns.
37. Be aware of the image you project—first impressions are important.
38. Take a long deep breath, look at the attendees, and then start to speak.
39. Your opening lines should capture their interest and should set the tone for your presentation.
40. Briefly explain what you will be talking about and how and why it's important to them.
41. Use examples from your experience and be convincing.
42. Allow participants to disagree with you; then explain why you believe differently.
43. If you can't answer a question, ask that the participant to come back to you at the end of the presentation for further discussion.

Concluding With Class

44. End on a positive note.

45. Reiterate your main points and summarize.

46. Inform them about available information on the topic (for example, brochures and books available at the back of the room).

47. Ask for feedback.

48. Look for non-verbal feedback.

49. Direct them to your website/email address (if appropriate).

50. Thank them for their participation.

The goals of effective presentations are to inform and influence. The style and approach you adopt while making presentations will evolve with time as you learn new approaches and ways of presenting information. With experience, your level of stress will diminish greatly and you will feel more comfortable being yourself. Look for feedback, whether verbal or non-verbal, and adjust your presentations accordingly.

Hear the Applause. You're On!

You can reduce your anxieties by ensuring that all will go according to the plan. So when you are being introduced, you can simply stand back and absorb the energy of the room. Memorable presentations are not accidents, they are carefully planned.

Only fools would dare to stand and make a presentation on a topic of which they know little or nothing. You should know your material well and anticipate the questions you are likely to get. A dry run with friends or colleagues may be useful to put you to the test.

On the day of the presentation, always arrive early enough to check the room and the audio-visual equipment. Make adjustments that will allow for the optimal performance. The following **Critical Success Factors 12-Step Checklist** will help you ensure that nothing major will go wrong. Once you are satisfied that the technical issues have been addressed, take time to meet some of the attendees in order to get a feel for your audience. Building rapport with your audience may be difficult once you are on the platform. So take advantage of those extra minutes prior to the presentation to forge links with participants. If appropriate, you may call upon them during your presentation to add personal experiences.

Critical Success Factors

Items to check	*Yes / No*	*Corrections to be made*
The laptop is plugged in and works properly.	_____	_____
The remote (or mouse) works properly.	_____	_____
A back-up hard copy of your presentation is available.	_____	_____
The image fits the screen and is in focus.	_____	_____
Electrical cords don't impede your movements.	_____	_____
Lighting is appropriate and does not flood the screen.	_____	_____
The podium does not hide the screen.	_____	_____
Microphones work properly (back-up is available).	_____	_____
The room layout suits your needs (no safety hazards).	_____	_____
The room has adequate ventilation.	_____	_____
Food and beverage tables are appropriately located.	_____	_____
Back-of-room tables are available.	_____	_____

Your visual presentation using PowerPoint™ or any other similar software should be easy to read (appropriate font style and size) with no more than five or six points (bullets) on each slide. The purpose of the slide is to draw the attention of the participant to the talking points. This is where your storytelling skills come in. Instead of reading the points, craft your message in a way that you tell a story by covering one or more points. Your audience will want to stay tuned as you move from one story to another and they cannot anticipate what you will say. Connect your stories with appropriate "segue."[2]

---

2. A "segue" (pronounced segway) is used to join together two different topics. Segues can be short or long. In some cases you may need to create a story that allows you to end one thought and introduce another. For example, a speaker on the issue of work/life balance was discussing the merits of having a circle of friends not connected to business concerns. The next point to be made was on the topic of the need to make time for personal non-work-related priorities. A segue was created by stating that having friends requires a time commitment to allow friendships to mature and grow and that this is a priority for many people, particularly for Generation Y individuals.

Interacting With Your Audience

Good leaders focus on the people they are trying to lead and/or manage. When making a presentation, remember that these people have come to hear you, and they expect that your message will be clear, concise, and will address their concerns. They must believe that you can help them, and it's your role to tell them what you can do for them and what they can do for themselves. The more convinced *you* are, the more convincing you will sound.

Your expertise in the subject matter will help answer questions as they arise. The longer you wait to answer, the more opportunity for a participant to tune out, or worse, to start chatting with another participant. Your credibility is directly linked to what people hear, and unless you're able to provide adequate answers, you will lose the interest and support of your participants. If these are your employees, it may affect your ability to lead.

If the material you are presenting is new to you, it would be wise to have attendees hold their questions until the end. In doing so, if you're running out of time, you can adjust the question-and-answer period to fill the time available. However, you will have completed your presentation, which was your primary objective. Should you not have enough time available for all questions, you may want to allow people to contact you via email.

Invariably, there will be one person who will ask a question that does not at all relate to your presentation. What should you do? Politely acknowledge the question, and if you can provide a very quick, non-intrusive answer, you may be able to diffuse the awkward moment. You may also consider asking the person to come and chat with you off-line at the next break. Avoid a one-on-one discussion that may be of interest to only that person, particularly when the question is off topic and the answer is unlikely to benefit anyone else.

Engaging the attendees by asking questions (e.g., *show of hands all of those who have lost their speaking notes just before a presentation*) is helpful in getting attention, but don't overdo it as participants don't typically learn much from this approach. Consider varying participant engagement by asking for testimonials or experiences. This can be done in a plenary session or in sub-groups. You can also engage participants by looking directly at them (individually and collectively) in such a way that you convey sincerity in your message. In small groups (30 or fewer), learning everyone's name is very useful. By using a person's name, imbedded in your replies to questions, the participant will spring to attention and will appreciate the personal touch. Name plates/name tags can be very useful for this purpose. On the rare occasions where you may be losing control of a group, using people's names will allow you to command more respect from them and they, in turn, will feel obliged to respect the group dynamics.

Final Thoughts

According to William Hewlett, co-founder of Hewlett-Packard, "the ability to clearly communicate ideas to clients and colleagues is a rare skill, yet one that often makes the difference in whether or not a great concept succeeds." It doesn't take the skills of a Greek orator like Demosthenes to make effective presentations; however, leaders need to learn the fundamentals of making effective presentations if they are to succeed in our fast-paced world. Every effort should be made to prepare yourself to give the best performance possible.

Every day, in every city, thousands of leaders are making presentations of every style and approach. Few of these will be remembered for any length of time. You can substantially increase your business or improve your career impact and prospects as a leader by making powerful, memorable presentations. Not only will people remember what you have said, they will also tell others about your skills. Word of mouth is your best advertising. Even if you only do presentations on an ad hoc basis, effective presentation skills will make you stand out from the crowd, thus increasing your opportunities for recognition and promotion.

Stand up and take a bow!

Charles Seems

Charles Seems is a seasoned human resources consultant, public speaker and writer with 25 years of experience. Under the banner of his company HR Spectrum, Charles offers "quality services to help you build the life you want," providing individual and group consultations on human resources management and team building issues. Based on a holistic perspective on life, Charles Seems speaks on issues dealing with personal success in the workplace and effective training delivery. His clients include large and small organizations in both the public and private sectors.

Charles is a graduate of l'Université de Moncton, the University of Ottawa and l'Université du Québec à Hull. A member of the Canadian Authors Association, Charles is the author of *Drug-Free Arthritis: Secrets to Successful Living* (2006) and is currently writing another book, tentatively entitled "Staffing 101: A Guide to Public Sector Employment," due to be released in 2008.

Business Name:	HR Spectrum
Address:	85 Bronson Avenue, Suite 504, Ottawa, ON K1R 6G7
Telephone:	613-237-3580
Email:	charo@sympatico.ca
Web Address:	www.CharlesSeems.com

Dawn Frail

Eagle Vision Leadership Development Group

The Ten Commandments of Ethical Leadership

Every company wants a competitive advantage. Every company wants to maximize profits and minimize costs. Every company wants to be innovative with their products and services while being prudent with risk. How do you manage these demands and stay at the top in your customers' hearts and minds?

The key to making this happen lies in your leadership team and in the very characters of the leaders themselves. If you have a leadership team that acts with integrity, you have the potential to build a powerhouse organization. The key is to have a team of ethical leaders. And this starts with you in your role as leader.

The Strategic Alignment Model—affectionately known as SAM—is a systematic approach to learning and applying the Ten Commandments of Ethical Leadership. SAM has four elements and within these fall the Ten Commandments put into an implementation framework. The SAM model helps you to systematically plan a series of actions that will build your leadership character from the inside out, reveal your unique leadership abilities, and also strengthen them.

The Need for SAM

What makes SAM so needed in the world today? One of the greatest losses in modern business is ethics. Some people and organizations still hold the belief that ethical behavior is bad for business. There may be a short-term boon to revenue through actions that challenge what really is ethical, but in the long run, profits cannot be maximized. You simply cannot sustain results that way.

One does not need to be the victim of a huge corporate scandal to feel the devastating effects of bad ethics. Consider a research and development department that cuts corners, spins stories, and controls contributors. What is the immediate impact to the people and productivity in that department? When ethics go by the wayside, products can become dangerous due to extreme cost-cutting, top talent starts to walk out the door because they feel taken advantage of, and people lose morale and stop giving 100 percent effort. They produce only enough to stay below the radar, wasting vast amounts of intellectual resources.

Now, think instead of how a company's results would be different if your people are led to make ethical choices and decisions that benefit both the customer and the company. People work harder and smarter when they are highly engaged. They rally around a worthwhile endeavor that leaves them feeling personally fulfilled at the end of the day. Communication becomes more open and honest, and conflict can be harnessed as creative energy. Teams work collaboratively because trust is enhanced both inside the team and interdepartmentally. Changes are implemented more quickly, and bottom-line productivity and profitability increase because of reduced resistance and stronger buy-in.

Meet the Strategic Alignment Model (SAM)

Now you're on board! How do you get these seemingly magical results? By putting SAM into practice and becoming a leader worth following. Meet SAM and the Ten Commandments of Ethical Leadership: SAM is an inside-out approach to leadership

development that begins by working on yourself in the role of leader. At the two foundational corners of SAM lie **Define You** and **Develop You**. If you expect to get change out of others, you must be willing to first change yourself. At the apex, or top, of the model is **Develop Others**, which you can only do if you have first laid a strong foundation. And at the center of the model is **Believe**—ensuring that the efforts you make come from faith in yourself and others.

Within these four elements of the Strategic Alignment Model are the Ten Commandments of Ethical Leadership. They fit as follows:

Define You

1. **Develop a Vision:** Know where you're going.
2. **Characterize Integrity:** Define who you are.
3. **Lead by Example:** Courageously demonstrate what you stand for.

Develop You

4. **Esteem Insight:** Discover your true strengths, weakness, gifts and talents.
5. **Love Learning:** Commit to effective, lifelong learning.
6. **Guard Your Heart:** Build emotionally intelligent intestinal fortitude.

Develop Others

7. **Invest Wisely:** Protect your most precious resource—your time.
8. **Exercise Humility:** Treat others with utmost respect, dignity and value.
9. **Leverage Loyalty:** Build trust and loyalty through servant leadership.

Believe

10. **Believe:** Have faith.

Let's look at each of these four elements and the Ten Commandments in greater detail.

Element #1—Define You

1. Develop a Vision

The first commandment requires you to develop a clear, concise and articulate vision of where you or your team is headed. Much of the power is in the *developing,* which is the hard work you'll go through to figure out exactly what you want the future to look like.

Along with a vision are a mission, a strategy, and a tactical plan. While organizations may have their own terms for these, an organization that doesn't have a clear picture of where it wants to go and how it will get there will never arrive. As a leader, if you don't know where you're going, you're going to have a hard time convincing anyone to come along with you.

A vision statement inspires people to want to come along for the ride. If it's too long and wordy, people won't be able to remember it; and if it's not clear, they'll be confused by it. The vision statement acts like true north on a compass: it helps a team keep its bearings. When the team gets off course, the vision reminds them where they ultimately want to go and helps them get back on track.

When developing your vision, be sure to involve others. If you want to maximize buy-in and reduce resistance, get as many people involved as is reasonable. By doing this you'll also be creating a team of champions sprinkled throughout the organization that will help you communicate the vision and set the example.

2. Characterize Integrity

The second commandment is about defining the characteristics of integrity based on your most important values. Values are the ideas and beliefs we hold about what is right and what is wrong. The problem with integrity, truth and values is that there is no right or wrong. What is "right" to one person (or organization, or country) can be "wrong" to another. In order to call yourself an ethical leader, you must know what *you* mean by integrity.

To characterize integrity you must define what your *key* values are. In other words, define the ones that are most important to you. After that, you can begin to understand what's behind the decisions you make, and then you can create a framework for making future decisions. Once you're able to do that, you'll find that even when you must make the tough decisions, you will still be at peace with yourself and able to sleep with a clear conscience.

To help you define your values, visit www.dawnfrail.com and look for the *Values Clarification Activity*. This activity will help you prioritize your most important values. Use the list you make as a magnifying glass to look more closely at your decisions and to help you make more ethical choices.

In defining your values, listen to your heart and select the values that are the most important to *you*, and not ones that society, colleagues, and those personally closest to you reinforce over the years. Don't worry about getting it right—if it's right for you, it's right.

3. Lead by Example

The third commandment requires you to take a look at your actions to be sure they line up with your words. As an ethical leader, it is critical that you determine what you stand for, and then make sure that your actions tell the same tale. Sometimes you need to look to your actions first to figure out what you really stand for. It's easy to say what you think you'd do if you were in a difficult situation. When actually faced with one, would you be able to follow through?

When it comes to defining who you are, your actions will tell more about you than anything you say. People will take their cue from you about what is acceptable behavior by the way you treat others at all levels within your organization. They'll learn as they watch how you get along with difficult peers and unruly customers.

A simple fact of leadership is that someone is always watching, so you are always setting an example. The question is whether you are setting the example you intend to set. People can only see and learn from what you do, and not what you intend to do.

Now that you've established a benchmark, it's time to raise the bar. Next, plan to take some very specific actions to develop and strengthen your leadership style.

Element #2—Develop You

4. Esteem Insight

The fourth commandment is about diving deep into who you really are and not being afraid to uncover your strengths and weaknesses. The single most important thing you can do to develop yourself is to discover what your true, natural gifts and talents are, and then focus your growth within those areas.

When you tap into your natural gifts and talents, great results come much more easily, activities are more fun, and you work with much less stress. To help you explore what your natural talents might be, ask yourself these questions:

- What games did you play as a child?
- What do you love to do so much that you'd do it for free?
- When your life is really, really busy, what can you always make time for?
- What job have you held that felt more like play than work?
- What do you do that leaves you feeling energized, fulfilled and peaceful?
- What gives you the greatest sense of accomplishment?
- When have you learned something new almost effortlessly?
- If you could do anything with your life, what would it be?

There are many tools that can help you, and in my practice I use the Myers-Briggs Type Indicator®. This tool assesses and assists you to understand underlying personality patterns and appreciate the differences in other people's personalities. Using this tool enhances communication and teamwork, reduces stress and conflict, and increases innovation and productivity.

5. Love Learning

The fifth commandment is about realizing and embracing the fact that learning is a lifelong journey. If there is such a thing as job security in the twenty-first century, then it lies in your ability to unlearn and relearn quickly. With the world changing so rapidly, this is definitely not a time to rest on your laurels. What made you successful in the past is unlikely to make you successful in the future. So be ready, willing and able to learn new ways to do old things.

When it comes to learning quickly, each person has their own natural and preferred learning style. When you seek out learning situations that match your style, you'll comprehend faster, retain more, and have more fun in the process. It can be difficult to let go of the old ways of doing things. Humans are creatures of habit, and old habits die hard.

As an ethical leader, you have to remind yourself that it's not that the "old way" is wrong, but that the times that made that "old way" right have changed, making it time for a different way.

Your ideas of right and wrong, good and bad, and success and failure are all tied up in an emotional bow when it comes to dealing with change. Like it or not, you need to keep learning or you will become obsolete. Not a pretty picture! Commit to a lifelong journey of learning, and you'll have all the career security you want.

6. Guard Your Heart

The sixth commandment is about developing emotional courage and not taking it personally when you come up against opposition. The things you "take to heart" will play a big role in how successfully you demonstrate your integrity. As an ethical leader, you'll stick your neck out on more than one occasion and risk getting your hand slapped. That's the life that you choose when you choose this path.

Even when you do the right thing, people will call you names and threaten you with some pretty nasty things. Do you remember the wrath of your so-called school friends when they thought you ratted them out to the teacher? Well, organizations are just like big playgrounds full of bullies. The only difference is that we're all in bigger bodies and the stakes are higher.

Organizations would oftentimes prefer to sweep the embarrassing situations under the rug and keep them quiet rather than give light to any questionable situation that might damage their reputation or their revenue. Whether you are standing up for the rights of an employee who has been mistreated or a customer who has been treated unfairly, there are times when the rest of the organization will want you to keep quiet. When you won't comply, they'll accuse you of not being a team player and may try to ostracize you into compliance. Learn to develop a thick skin and let the negative stuff slide right off your back. If you take the insults to heart, you let it change you. If you let others convince you that you're stupid because you chose to do the right thing, your ethical journey will be a short one. So don't let anyone knock you off your path.

As you develop your skills, play to your strengths, and perhaps even quit that well-paying job that makes you miserable, some people in your life won't like it. Sadly, the closer the people are to you, the more resistant they can be to your change. Give people time and stand your ground. Learn to manage change and help others accept the change that you've chosen to make.

Now that you have taken a good, critical look at who you are, and you've found the areas where you want to develop your leadership skills and style, you have earned the right to ask others to do the same. By learning to lead yourself effectively, you earn the right to lead others.

Element #3—Develop Others

7. Invest Wisely

The seventh commandment is about making smart decisions regarding how and where you will invest your most precious resource: your time. Remember, whatever else is going on, your team is your most important commitment.

It's a wise investment to spend time helping, directing, leading and motivating your team because it yields exponential results. It's the "teach a person to fish" concept: It's smarter to teach your team to fish so they can fish for themselves each day than to return every day to give them more fish.

Let the tasks that team members are working on dictate the amount of time you spend with them. If you assign a new task, spend more time with those people while they are learning and becoming more confident. For other tasks, where they have gone from learning mode to doing mode, devote less individual time. Be sure that your team understands your leadership style when it comes to deciding who will get your individual attention. You risk being accused of favoritism if you don't.

The key to time management is to focus on one thing at a time. Keep your time in blocks as best you can because fractions of minutes are too hard to manage. Minimize how often you switch between tasks, because the more you switch back and forth, the more momentum and energy is wasted. Recall the last time you were interrupted in the middle of an important task and found it difficult to get back into your groove.

8. Exercise Humility

The eighth commandment is about having a high value, respect and honor for other people and treating them as though they are very important—no matter who they are or what their place is in the organization's structure.

**Humility means to not be prideful, arrogant or power-hungry,
yet it's not about being meek and mild and rolling over either.
You can be both humble and a very powerful leader at the same time.**

Leadership Gurus Speak Out!

It takes humility to help people develop, because it requires you to let go and let them do things their way. It takes a humble leader to be forgiving when a mistake is made, and to let them learn from their mistake. Delegating authority with responsibility and acknowledging that there are many right ways to do something takes great humility

You need humility to empower others so they learn, grow and succeed, and even more to help them succeed beyond your level to a place you might still be trying to reach. It takes humility to take more than your share of blame and give more than your share of credit. It takes humility to deliver feedback in a positive and motivating fashion and to give praise and thanks to others both for results and for efforts along the way. It takes a confident and humble leader to truly value diversity and to wholeheartedly embrace it.

9. Leverage Loyalty

The ninth commandment is about being a servant leader who takes care of the needs of their team so those people can then take care of the needs of the organization. It's about *being of service*, and you do this through a collaborative leadership style.

Servant leadership is not about you being subservient to your followers. It is instead about you taking the time to remove obstacles from their paths so they can be highly successful. How your team performs is a direct reflection on your ability as a leader. Think of yourself as the quarterback for your team. You will throw the ball to your team members so they can make touchdowns. That will happen far more often than you carrying the ball into the end zone yourself. That is the essence of servant leadership, and it builds loyalty.

Don't think that you'll have to trade business results for niceness. As a good leader, you know that the way to make money is through the efforts of many other people. You can't possibly do it all yourself. Instead, you have to try to get more and/or better work out of the same people and hopefully increase profits at the same time.

Having a "being of service" perspective is the foundation of relational leadership. The relationships you have with your people are based on the strength of the trust that exists between you. Trust is a precursor to loyalty, and loyalty is the single most profitable element in your business mix. That's because loyalty can be leveraged—a little bit of it will yield you a high rate of return.

Element #4—Believe

10. Believe!

Believing is the fourth element—and the Tenth Commandment—to the Strategic Alignment Model. It is the foundational energy for the model to be effective; it is about having faith in and expecting a positive outcome. "To believe" is at the center of the Strategic Alignment Model and a source of strength for you as a leader. Anything you can believe in your heart, see in your mind, and generate an emotional attachment to, is virtually guaranteed to be yours. There are four things that you need to believe in:

1. **You need to believe in a higher power.** Whoever or whatever you call God would certainly fit into this category. If you don't have a God-of-choice, then you need to decide what higher power you do believe in. Some people simply believe that there is "something bigger than just me." Know what gives you inner strength and know from where you draw your faith.

2. **You need to believe in your people.** You need to believe they are good and that they deserve the very best you have to offer. You need to believe they want to learn and grow and perform. You need to believe they are self-motivated and that your job is to inspire them to be the very best they can be.

3. **You need to believe in your company and the products or services that it provides.** You need to believe that you provide value to the lives of the people you call your customers, and that it's not only about lining the pockets of a select few. You need to have pride in your organization and find meaning and satisfaction in the job you do.

4. **Most important, you need to believe in yourself.** You need to believe you are capable and deserving and good. You need to believe you have something to offer your employer, your family, and your community. You need to know perfection is neither attainable nor desirable, and that your real goal should be the pursuit of excellence.

Activating the Strategic Alignment Model

Now that you have a clear picture of what SAM is all about and how the Ten Commandments of Ethical Leadership fit into the model, it's time to decide what you want to do with it. Each of us has different leadership development needs, so you need to look at SAM with a critical eye to determine what your best implementation strategy will be.

However you decide to proceed, the main thing is that you *do* proceed. Once you begin, know that it's a never-ending journey. To become and remain a strong ethical leader takes discipline. SAM isn't something you'll go through once and then check off your to-do list, never to revisit it. Like many things in life, it's a cycle. You'll want to periodically **Define You** by looking at what's important and taking a critical look at how you measure up to your own standards. You'll continuously look for ways to **Develop You** by learning new skills and growing in the areas where your natural talents lie, as well as the areas that interest you. You'll always be on the lookout for ways to **Develop Others** by making sure you invest your resources wisely, and that you put relationships with your people at the top of your priority list.

By following the Ten Commandments of Ethical Leadership, you will find results are better, people are more productive, and your company is delivering higher value to customers, employees and shareholders. There is no doubt it will flow directly to your bottom line. But remember that for every positive action there is an evil twin. If you don't follow the steps to become an ethical leader, and choose instead to engage in activities that are authoritarian or dictatorial, these will also flow detrimentally to the bottom line.

In the long run, there is only one way to sustain profitable growth in your organization, and that's by doing right by people—all people. Since what's *right* isn't always obvious, there are many traps that await you. If my words resonate with you and your intention is to implement some, or all, of this model, you are a leader with great potential to make a difference in the world. The world needs more leaders like you—ones who are willing to do what is right, when it is right, and for the right reason. Your efforts are being applauded and success is waiting for you around the corner. Go meet it!

Dawn Frail

Dawn Frail inspires leaders to build trust and loyalty so their teams will increase productivity and profits. She helps leaders and organizations achieve these dynamic results by creating a powerful leadership team—from the inside out. Timeless wisdom is brought to life for you and your organization through interactive workshops, seminars and keynotes.

Through her research on ethics and leadership, Dawn's mission is to help leaders understand that it is highly profitable to behave ethically. As she focuses her expertise on women in leadership, it is her personal goal to help women break the glass ceiling and enter the senior leadership ranks in their organizations.

Dawn is the author of *Powerful Presentation Skills, Powerful Presentation Skills for Women* and *10 Principles Every CEO Must Know to Play and Win.* Audio presentations include *Simple Secrets of Success, The Ethical Advantage* and *Rules Are Made to Be Broken.*

Dawn holds a diploma in Adult Training and Development from the University of Toronto and is a certified Myers-Briggs® practitioner.

Business Name:	Eagle Vision Leadership Development Group
Address:	5 Whitney Way, Caledon, ON L7K 1H7
Telephone:	519-927-1730
Email:	dawn@dawnfrail.com
Web Address:	www.dawnfrail.com
Professional Affiliations:	Canadian Association of Professional Speakers; Canadian Society of Training and Development

Lesley Southwick-Trask

AskLesley.Com

The Holographic Leader: New Era, New Models, New Leadership

If you are like most leaders, you have done your fair share of strategic planning and change work. You have undoubtedly participated in countless sessions and meetings dutifully responding to and analyzing surveys and scans designed to blueprint the future. Have you ever stopped to wonder why so much effort is invested in predicting futures that realize at best 30 percent of what has been planned? Change management, strategic planning and organizational development represent bodies of work that served our society well over the past three decades. The question is whether their respective theories and practices rooted in twentieth century dynamics have outlasted their usefulness? My answer is yes.

But you already know this. How? Your frustration and fatigue with recycled strategic plans and chronic change management issues has sparked your search for any methods and techniques that can transcend the cause and effect thinking and circular programming with innate wisdom and inspired action. What I am introducing in this chapter is the twenty-first century alternative to the tired and overused theories that have outlived their prime in the developed world. In the same manner that the nineteenth century manufacturing plant manager replaced the overseeing of manual labour in farmlands, fisheries and sail-powered trade, so does the holographic leader replace the industrial manager. Holographic leadership represents our innate capabilities that can naturally identify, interpret and take action on the complex issues shaping the present and the future. These inherent techniques not only enable real-time movement on issues traditionally addressed by strategic planning, change management, and organizational development theories; they replace generalized thinking with precise, targeted action.

What Does Holographic Mean?

Most of us were introduced to the concept of holographs in the film *Star Wars* when R2D2 produced a life-like image of Princess Leia. The eerie extension of Princess Leia was the result of a complex series of refracted light images placed onto photographic film and then projected into space. "But what has this got to do with leadership?" you must be asking yourselves. The relevancy comes with the adaptation of quantum science to the world of leadership. In the same manner that Margaret Wheatly and other leadership experts have applied theories such as strange attractors (magnetic fields in the vortex of tornados) and fractals (nature's form of imprinting the whole in the part) to modern day leadership (strange attractors—the unprecedented growth of unpredictable trends—and fractal systems—values as part of every action) holography provides a new lens with which to experience our dynamic world. Holographs store the entire image into every part.

Translated into leadership terms, the most basic application of holography in today's organization is the popularized concept of the power of one that positions every person as a leader. Such a theory becomes viable only when each individual (part) embodies the organization's vision, values, and cultural underpinnings (the whole). In this way, it can be said that the whole is embodied in every part. This approach to leadership is critical in a world in which the most significant determinants of success are navigated, negotiated, and shaped by those with the greatest exposure to the field—the front line.

In an environment in which the market, public and customer define and control the rules of the game, success is only possible through a dynamic network of people who are empowered to act as holographic representatives of the CEO—embodying the same vision, values, beliefs and situational competence as the prime leader.

In this manner, the symbiotic relationship between the needs of those seeking products and services with those empowered to serve these needs are held at the immediate point where contact is made. At that very moment, the political, environmental, economic and social conditions navigated by the executive officers come to life in the decision making of this exchange. In a quantum world, this trade is a microcosm of the market rather than merely the end point of an engineered flow chart depicting the sales cycle.

Does the power of one mean that an organization is simply a cluster of CEO clones? The answer is undeniably "no." But to provide meaning to this response, we have to go to a deeper understanding of the human being as a holograph— a dynamic field of energy frequencies. Let's start this exploration with you taking a look at your hand. I am sure that you see the same thing you always do—skin covering bones, muscles, nerves and tissue. But what if you had microscopic vision and were able to go into the cells that make up your hand? You would find cells that hold the blueprint for the entire body, while having the specialized function of the hand. These cells are surrounded by an energy field holding a vast amount of information. Each of us has seven major energy fields and a number of minor ones. I am referring to chakras which are centers of activity that receive, assimilate, and express life force energy. The word *chakra* literally translates as *wheel* or *disk* and refers to a spinning sphere of bioenergetic activity emanating from the major nerve ganglia branching forward from the spinal column. There are seven of these wheels stacked in a column of energy that spans from the base of the spine to the top of the head. There are also minor chakras in the hands, feet, fingertips and shoulders. The seven major chakras correlate with basic states of consciousness.

But what has this got to do with leadership? In order to see its relevancy to us as leaders, we need to own the belief system we currently hold about people. Throughout history, humans have been viewed predominately as physical beings designed to survive amidst the ever-changing environmental landscape. The industrial era brought with it the view that man was simply an extension of the machine. For those of us born before 1981, logic and rational thinking, coupled with Newtonian principles of power and control, have dominated the way in which we have perceived, and interacted with the world and how we perceive others and ourselves. The reality that we are actually energy—and not logic—challenges us and our core beliefs about our work, how we lead, and those whom we lead.

Over the past twenty years, we have (painfully) undertaken our departure from the industrial economy and movement into the knowledge economy. This has brought a fundamental shift in all aspects of our society, including our notion of people.

While the tail end of the industrial era saw the slogan of people as "our greatest resource" tossed around, the knowledge economy has awakened the perspective that society exists exclusively in and through human intelligences and energies. This fundamental shift in how we view the human factor is obviously central to a new way of leading. To truly understand this phenomenon, we need to take a closer look at our beliefs surrounding the nature and role of leadership.

The challenge facing leaders today resides in the mental models and belief systems that are replacing the industrialized tenants, most of which appear invisible to those of us raised in them. We have come to assume that big is better; positional power influences others; business leads the way; politicians determine the future; the gross national product is a true indication of prosperity; people work to job descriptions; what we do is more important than who we are; and jobs and personal lives are to be balanced. These are eight of the hundreds of beliefs and principles that no longer run the show in terms of knowledge-society thinking and decision making.

When we combine the concepts of the whole living in every part (holography) and human beings as wheels of life-force energies (chakras), we start to perceive a different leadership landscape. We begin to realize that leadership in the knowledge economy is a great deal more than empowering and enabling people to achieve a common vision amidst double-digit growth of technology, Internet-enabled networks and computerized wisdom. We are beginning to awaken to the magnificence of the human condition—our physical, emotional, mental and spiritual energies that become intertwined and incorporated as one life force or chi. Most of us are early-stage learners about the potential that we hold. The power to see beyond our eyes, feel beyond our reach, and know more than what our lifetime has taught us is at our immediate disposal. Scientists such as Karl Jung and John Chilton Pearce confirm that it is simply a matter of consciousness.

When we allow ourselves to truly embrace the larger electromagnetic energy field that is both an information center and an advanced perceptual system (we can "see, feel, believe and act" in a more precise manner), we start to realize that we are constantly in communication with everything around us through our transmission and receipt of messages to and from other people's energy systems. Think of this as an updated version of the communication theory that we pick up only 5 percent of what we hear through the words that people use.

The call for the outer expression of deep-seated innate power is being made. Leadership in today's world is about recognizing, unleashing and mobilizing these innate powers as a means of addressing the ever-increasing complexity of issues, dynamics and opportunities facing today's organizations and communities. We have moved from the silo and separate thinking of the Industrial Age depicted in the prevailing advice to "separate the person from the problem" to the holographic notion that if you are not part of the problem, you cannot be part of the solution.

Central to these principles is the belief that the future is not a destination, but rather a reality that already exists, waiting to be uncovered. The holographic universe goes one step further. Its premise is that the world as we know it is comprised of energetic frequencies, each of which operates with their own purpose, function and information. In the same way that each human cell holds the blueprint of the entire body, so does each human being embody these universal frequencies. Embedded in these frequencies is our individual DNA—a codified form of information unique to each human being. Encrypted in our DNA is our distinct source of wisdom that only we have the ability to decode and unleash as our exclusive contribution to the evolution of the world. It is with this insight that we are able to understand the statement made famous by Gandhi: "We must be the change we wish to see in the world."

Preparing the Mind

So how does this really work? How can a leader work with these human frequencies so as to realize prosperity for one's community, one's organization, one's teams, and oneself? Let's find out. The rest of this chapter is dedicated to helping you to get in touch with your own frequencies and their inherent information designed to guide your leadership. Becoming familiar with your own powers will enable you to open up your thinking to the conditions that will sponsor the unleashing, interpreting and connecting of those frequencies belonging to the people with whom you have a leadership relationship. Alchemy—the ancient science of turning lead into gold—finds its modern day equivalent in the leadership strategy of taking ordinary human beings and transforming their frequencies into extraordinary leadership advice.

To begin this work, you must ready yourself. A decade ago this would have meant rolling up your sleeves and being ready to write up the flow of ideas generated from conceptually powered brainstorming. Today, preparation comes in the form of creating a quiet and relaxed state of mind.

Exercise

1. Sit quietly with your eyes either focused loosely on a point in front of you or closed.

2. Take three deep breaths through your nose and your mouth, focusing your attention on your diaphragm as it expands to take in the air.

3. Allow the air to leave through your nose and mouth, mindful of your diaphragm contracting. Allow yourself to experience the air entering your body as pure energy coming in to clean your system.

4. While you inhale, imagine the air moving through your entire system lightly scrubbing off the plague of tension wherever it is located.

5. As you exhale, witness the tension that is leaving with it.

6. Keep breathing in and out, focusing your attention lightly on areas in your body that hold tension—starting at your toes, then your heels, ankles, calves, knees, thighs and buttocks; continue up to your abdomen, your chest, small of your back, up your spinal cord, hands, palms, wrists, lower arms, elbows, upper arms, shoulders, shoulder blades, neck, chin, mouth, face, cheeks, forehead, ears, skull, and finally the top of your head. Remember to rest your attention gently on the parts of the body that you are cleaning with your breath.

7. Go back to those areas where the tension continues to lodge itself. Note where any area of tension remains when you are as relaxed as possible.

With your mind void of thoughts, you are ready for the next step:

8. While you softly maintain the rhythm of your breathing, allow a vision of the life to which you aspire to emerge. Permit yourself to experience the detail—people, colors, sounds and activities that are coming to life in your mind. Do not judge this vision or try to analyze it. Simply allow it to unfold in front of you. Let it find its way into your body—feel it, taste it, smell it, hear it, touch it, and see it.

9. Once you have embodied your vision, shift your experience to the organization or community you are leading. Allow your vision of the organization that you are aspiring to create, emerge. Again, allow it to simply unfold in all of its glory. Experience it in all of its detail. Once you have fully embraced the place, space and people alive in the aspired vision of your community or organization, quickly bring current reality into your consciousness. Experience it as a collision of vision meeting reality.

10. Immediately become aware of the place in your body where you are feeling the tension of the collision between your vision of your organization or community and current reality.

This is what we call the moment of truth in holographic leadership. You have now created the interference pattern that holds the greatest information that will best guide your leadership action at this point in time. It comes from using two dimensions—the vision of future and the reality of now—in the same manner as light beams collide to create holographic photography. In holographic terms this is actually the collision of your aspiration that already exists and is waiting to be discovered with the mental, physical, emotional and spiritual filters that are preventing this aspiration from being realized.

The Awakening of Inherent Wisdom

Now that we understand how we can create these collision points, let's look at the meaning behind them. As you learn to identify and assess these collision points, you'll be able assess and implement the wisdom that they provide. Information, direction and solution comes through "hearing" the wisdom of each of our primary

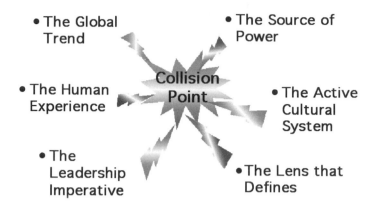

- The Global Trend
- The Source of Power
- The Human Experience
- Collision Point
- The Active Cultural System
- The Leadership Imperative
- The Lens that Defines

Figure 1: The General Frequencies

energetic centers—the seven chakras. While you are asked to pay particular attention to the collision point in which your vision/reality occurred, it will be important to note the other zones (chakras) and their implicit wisdom.

Each of these zones contains six discrete sources or frequencies:

The Global Trend: This is the channel that holds the master trends that are shaping the globe.

The Human Experience: This is the gateway to the conditions that enable human beings to function at their optimum.

The Source of Power: This is the frequency that takes us to the sources of significant power available for use.

The Active Cultural System: This is the channel that houses our socialized and often unconscious principles and practices that guide our everyday behavior.

The Lens That Defines: This frequency directs us in the perspectives that we are being asked to embrace by this collision point.

The Leadership Imperative: This frequency focuses us on the matters most requiring our attention concerning this collision point. This frequency directs us in the leadership we are being asked to embrace.

Now that we have an understanding of the general frequencies, let's take a look at what they mean, depending on where you experienced the collision point in the body. Take a moment to recall the place in your body where this tension occurred.

Zone 1: Roots—Your Survival Code

This energetic area (known as the Root Chakra) physically sits at the base of the spine at the tailbone in back, the pubic bone in front, hips, legs, feet, or lower back. Discomfort in this zone is indicative of a collision between your vision and the current reality you are experiencing. You have been drawn into this zone by your organization/community's basic needs for survival, security and safety. And if something is amiss with this, your physical awareness will be drawn to this area.

This is the center of manifestation. When you are trying to make things happen in the material world, in business, or in connection to material possessions, the energy to succeed will come from this first vortex. On a personal level, if this energy field becomes blocked, you can feel fearful, anxious, insecure and frustrated. Tension in this zone originates from one or more of the following:

- Your organization/community's sense of belonging in the market (i.e. positioning) or your members' feeling of belonging in the organization/community;
- Your economic viability;
- The essence of your work (such as what the calling it has for you and those you serve);
- What you see as your "turf"—i.e. your organizational/community boundaries (such as niches, market penetration, lines of authority, public/private offerings, etc.).

The questions listed below will help you glean more clarity as to your organization's or community's survival code—the area you have identified as being the most challenged at this present time. These questions have been designed to help you reach solutions for the tensions that are showing up in this zone. Tension in this area is suggesting that you place primary attention on uncovering the underlying **survival strategy** for grounding your organization or community for growth.

- What boundaries associated with your sense of security and impact on survival are changing?
- What will create a deeper sense of belonging amongst the members of your organization/community?
- What grounding and sense of well-being do you receive from your "roots" as an organization or community?

- What is the unique nature of your group's "tribal power"—that which binds you and defines you as a group?
- What is your organization or community uniquely capable of in terms of economic viability?
- What will it take for your organization or community to relate to the world in terms of who you are rather than what you do?

Zone 2: Connections—Your Relationship Code

Zone 2 (known as the Sacral Chakra) speaks to those who experienced the tension two inches below the navel either in the front or back of the body, which includes the sexual organs, kidneys, bladder and large intestines. This energy zone holds the basic needs for creativity, relationship and emotion. It governs your organization/community's confidence in its creativity, and its ability to build strong and intimate relationships. Proper balance in this center means the ability to flow with emotions freely and to feel and reach out to others. On a personal level, if this zone becomes blocked, you may feel emotionally explosive, manipulative, obsessed, or lack energy. Tension in this zone originates from one or more of the following:

- Important, yet challenging/conflict-riddled relationships;
- Distrust in key relationships, challenging you as you exchange vital information and know-how;
- Social structures that enable/disable the ability for your organization/community to meaningfully address challenges;
- Emotional intoxication, stagnation or distress;
- Struggles with true collaboration.

The questions below will help you know your organization's "relationship code." Tension in this area is suggesting that you place primary attention on uncovering the underlying **relationship strategy** designed to realize true prosperity.

- What relationships determine your organization/community's prosperity?
- How can you sponsor greater intimacy in your relationships?
- How do you best create connectivity with the world?
- How can you build legitimacy and vibrancy in your organization/community's emotional intelligence?

Leadership Gurus Speak Out!

- What structures would best enable prosperity?
- What opportunities do we see when we use the lenses of those born after 1981?

Zone 3: Abundance—Identity Code

This zone (known as the Solar Plexus Chakra) is located two inches below the breastbone in the center behind the stomach, which includes the stomach, liver, gall bladder, pancreas and small intestine. This energy zone is the center of personal power, the place of ego, of passions, impulses, anger and strength.

If you experience your tension in this area, it indicates that you are out of balance on a personal level. You may find yourself lacking confidence, becoming confused, worrying about what others think, and possibly feeling that others are controlling you. You may even become depressed. When this third zone is balanced you feel cheerful, outgoing, expressive and self-respectful. You can also experience a strong sense of personal power and are able to enjoy taking on new challenges. Tension in this zone originates from one or more of the following:

- Your organization/community's place and identity in a rapidly changing landscape;
- Your uniqueness as an organization/community and/or the manner in which you are offering it;
- Your organization/community's natural disposition to experiencing challenges through either constraint/restriction or abundance/openness with ideas, resources, opportunities, and so on;
- Your organization/community's autonomy as an intact society and the need for independence;
- Use of power and control by yourself or others.
- The manner in which decisions are being made and conflicts are being resolved.

Tension in this area is suggesting that you place primary attention on uncovering the underlying **branding strategy** designed to realize optimum positioning for prosperity. Refer to these questions to help with this process:

- How can you best leverage the diversity inherent in your organization/community's demographics?
- What is your organization/community's unique DNA—the brand you take out into the world?
- In what is your organization/community truly abundant?
- How can you link the personal power of your members to goals of prosperity?
- How can your group collectively make decisions and resolve conflicts in a manner that sponsors prosperity?
- How can you pass real power to your next generation of leaders?

Zone 4: Faith—Our Heart's Code

This is the zone (known as the Heart Chakra) for those who experienced tension in the area behind the breast bone in front and on the spine between the shoulder blades in the back. This zone includes the heart, lungs, circulatory system, shoulders, upper back, arms and hands. Here is the center of love, compassion and spirituality. This center directs one's ability to give and to receive love. This is also the energy zone that connects the body and mind with the spirit.

On a personal level, when this center goes out of balance we can feel sorry for ourselves, even paranoid, indecisive, afraid of letting go, afraid of getting hurt, or unworthy of love. When this energy zone is balanced we feel compassionate, friendly and empathetic, and experience a desire to nurture others and see the good in everyone. Tension in this zone originates from one or more of the following:

- Issues surrounding faith in the system in which you are playing a key part;
- The nature of how your organization/community balances giving and taking; personal and professional demands; divisions between work and home;
- Questions about respect amongst key groups of people;
- Your organization/community's beliefs and the manner in which they are actually exercised;
- Compassion and passion and the role these play in your organization/community;
- What your organization/community truly values.

Tension in this area is suggesting that you place primary attention on **uncovering the underlying belief strategy** designed to realize the glue that keeps your organization/community together. To help explore your organization's "heart code," refer to the following questions. These questions will help you explore your own or your organizations' belief strategy:

- How can your organization/community operate as an efficient and effective society in its own right?
- What belief(s) hold the greatest power for your organization/community?
- What vision does your organization/community hold that would mobilize collective action?
- How can you more fully sponsor the energy of love as an organization/community?
- What are your organization/community's universal values that can act as the glue to hold your group together?
- What change in what belief holds the tipping point of your transformation?

Zone 5: True Expressions—Osmosis Code

This is the zone (also known as the Throat Chakra) where people experience tension in their throat. This energy zone is located in the V of the collarbone at the lower neck and is the center of communication, sound, and expression of creativity via thought, speech and writing. It includes the throat, neck, teeth, ears and thyroid gland.

The possibility for change, transformation and healing are located here. The throat is where anger is stored and released. On a personal note, when this center is out of balance we may feel timid, want to hold back, become quiet, feel weak, or become unable to express our thoughts. When we feel balanced in this area, we can feel musically or artistically inspired, and may find ourselves able to openly express our inner most thoughts. Tension in this zone originates from one or more of the following:

- The presence or absence of authentic communication;
- Challenges with telling the truth. (You could be confused between the truth as you know it and what others want you to believe/say);

- Innovation, creativity and risk-taking as either natural, absent, or inconsistent/conflicting cultural dynamics throughout your organization/community;
- Heat in the dynamics associated with teaching others in what you have mastered;
- Coming to grips with where your organization/community is in this place in "time" and "being" on the "edge."

Tension in this area is suggesting that you place primary attention on uncovering the underlying **innovation and communications strategies** designed to realize prosperity. These questions can help uncover these strategies:

- How can you use cyberspace as the next creative frontier for your organization/community?
- What is the truth about you and your organization/community's relationship with prosperity that is waiting to be voiced?
- What must your organization/community become fearless about?
- What innovative idea is ready for "liftoff"—one with the greatest risk and return?
- What is the most difficult thing for your organization/community to communicate?
- How can your organization/community foster and embrace many types of intelligence to stimulate your path to prosperity?

Zone 6: Invisible—Our Starlight Code

This is the zone for people who experienced their tension in the Third Eye Chakra—the center of the forehead. The eyes, face, brain, spinal column, lymphatic and endocrine systems form this energy zone. This is the center for psychic ability, higher intuition, the energies of spirit and light. On a personal level, it assists in the purification of negative tendencies and in the elimination of selfish attitudes. When this zone is not balanced, we may feel non-assertive or afraid of success, or go the opposite way and become egotistical. When we are balanced and open in this area, we become our own master with no fear of death and without attachment to material things. Tension in this zone originates from one or more of the following:

- What it means to be an attractive workplace—including recruitment and retention of talent;
- The mental models and world views that provide clarity, direction and confidence for your organization or community;
- How reality comes in and out of focus, including patterns of thinking and ranges of feelings experienced by you and your members;
- What success really looks like—at least in terms of what you can feel proud of achieving and confident in your ability to realize;
- The role and use of technology and its applications including the advanced technology of the mind and the body in addition to computers, scientific equipment, and manufacturing machinery.

Tension in this area is suggesting that you place primary attention on uncovering the **strategy of the invisible** that targets those forces quietly and implicitly, underpinning success. The following questions will help explore your organization/community's Starlight Code.

- What are you willing to let die in order to open up the new growth?
- What are you "awakening" to in terms of new prosperity?
- What invisible mental blocks or models define/impact everything?
- Whose power of the mind must you tap into?
- What is your organization/community's most leading edge technology?
- What magnet can your organization/community use to attract prosperity?

Zone 7: Renewal—Our Umbilical Code

This is the zone for people who experienced their tension in the crown (Crown Chakra) located just behind the top of the skull. This is the center of spirituality, enlightenment, dynamic thought, and energy. It allows for the inward flow of wisdom and the gift of universal consciousness. This is also the center of connectedness with a higher source of power, and the place where life animates the physical body. On a personal level, when this energy zone becomes unbalanced we experience frustration and lack joy, and harbor destructive feelings. Balanced energy in this area provides the ability to open up to the unconscious and subconscious. Tension in this zone originates from one or more of the following:

- Where your organization/community is naturally headed at this point in time (Up? Down? Stuck? Racing?);
- The nature of the organizational/community goals (Paper tigers? Real and authentic? Easy or challenging? Inclusive or exclusive?
- Having a sense of being deeply committed to a purpose as an organization or community;
- Knowing where the organization/community stands in terms of its future aspirations;
- What it takes to experience joy and spontaneity, contentment/discontentment; satisfaction/dissatisfaction;
- Staying interested in things on a sustained basis;
- Getting ready to make some bold decisions on direction;
- The ability to focus on the "now" rather than having the organization/community's head in either the past of the future.

You are able to explore your organization/community's Umbilical Code through the questions outlined below. Tension in this area is suggesting that you place primary attention on uncovering the **strategy for bold growth** that targets the arenas that are holding the greatest energy for change:

- How can our organization/community sponsor a true sense of freedom?
- Where in our organization/community is the greatest clash of growth?
- What gives us a true sense of power to make things better?
- What story or events, already in motion, describe our pathway to prosperity?
- What discomfort can be turned into exhilaration in order to move forward?
- How can we use polarization in our organization/community to open to prosperity?

Moving to Action

Know that this is a process of shifting your patterns of thinking, feeling, believing and doing. It takes time and patience and at times is hard work. But shift it you must. Engage people of like minds. Engage even more of those who do not share the same thinking as you. By definition, they are holding a different piece of the puzzle. Be bold in who you invite to the table to do this work with you.

Remember, alchemy—the task of changing the ordinary into the extraordinary—will not come on a silver platter. It will take courage and conviction. It will require going from words to action. The outcome, however, is pure magic.

Lesley Southwick-Trask

Lesley Southwick-Trask is president of Southwick-Trask Holdings, a group of companies committed to supporting leaders, their teams, organizations and communities in their discovery and realization of their destiny—strategic, operational and cultural. As a modern-day cultural anthropologist, Lesley has repositioned hundreds of organizations and communities involving thousands of change interventions using a range of targeted innovative tools and methodologies. CEOs and their leadership teams engage Lesley when either their present or their future appears challenging and complex. Lesley's unique approach to transformation blends the social and physical sciences with modern western business acumen and ancient transformational wisdom. These powerful intervention tools enable her to co-create formulas with her clients that capture the hearts, minds and spirit of the people who hold the future of the organization in their hands.

Lesley's work has been highly recognized. She holds the award of one of the Top 100 Most Powerful Women in Canada in the category of Entrepreneur (by the Women's Executive Network in association with the Richard Ivey School of Business and the *Globe and Mail*), as well as a Trailblazer—a once-in-a-lifetime recognition. These awards followed her recognition as one the Top 50 CEOs in Atlantic Canada and one of the Top 100 Women Business Owners in Canada by *Profit Magazine* and *Chatelaine*. Lesley has been recognized as one of 25 people who are "Changing the Face of Halifax," as well as one of Atlantic Canada's leading thinkers by *Progress Magazine*.

As a writer, Lesley is probably best known for *Turning It Around: How Ten Canadian Organizations Changed Their Fortune*, a book she co-authored with Eva Innes for the *Financial Post*. Her articles have been published in the *Globe and Mail* and the *National Post*, and her commentary has been sought by a range of TV and radio hosts.

These accomplishments, however, only hold meaning when placed in relationship to her role as mother to five grown children—a role she shares with her life and business partner, Greg Trask.

Business Name:	Ask Lesley.Com
Address:	360 Crows Nest Drive, Halifax, NS B3H 3X5
Telephone:	902-420-9630
Email:	Lesley@asklesley.com
Web Address:	www.asklesley.com
Professional Affiliations:	WXN Top 100 & Mentor, Canadian Association of Professional Speakers, Dalhousie Continuing Medical Education

Pat Mussieux

Purple People Leaders

Charting Your Course

If today one more woman learns how great she really is,
then for me it has been a great day!

Mary Kay Ash

It was a sunny summer day and I was sitting on the patio at Earl's Restaurant in Edmonton, Alberta, along with my gal pals. A group, we met regularly to socialize, to encourage, to support, to share, and to laugh. We had all been in the work world, in different jobs, at various levels, for many years. (I was working under contract with a post-secondary institution.) Over the years, we dreamt of finding a way that we could pool, and use, our diverse talents and experiences for the direct benefit of young women climbing the corporate ladder. It was a conversation we had frequently.

On this particular day, my friends gave me a "call to action." As I was in an influential leadership position, it was time for me to make it happen. "The Leadership Institute for Young Career Women" was created as a two-year certificate program, for young women between the ages of 25 and 35. The focus was on soft skills training—much of it being the real-life skills that we, as the "senior generation," had to go and learn for ourselves. And many of these were the key elements of effective leadership.

In this chapter I am focusing on leadership for women, especially for those who are in the early stages of their careers. Whether you are a woman leader, or are leading women, you will learn proven techniques and tools. If you want to become an authentic, effective, progressive individual, this information is for you! My fundamental interest is for each of you to develop your critical thinking to create the best career possible. The information is presented in a two-step format. Working with these strategies each day will enable you, or your staff, to really internalize them.

Taking Charge of Personal Development

Do self-doubt, perfectionism and procrastination haunt you in spite of your achievements (or even, perhaps, because of them)? Failure, or even the fear of failure, can be paralyzing. Yet, failure is not the disaster we've come to believe it to be. By embracing and examining "failure," we find the key ingredients to our success. So where do we begin?

How the Mind Works

It is essential to know that present thoughts determine future results. It all starts with the way you think. As Lou Tice explains in his book *A Better World, A Better You*:

> *A widely accepted way to look at the process of thought has been in terms of the conscious and subconscious. Occasionally, a third is added—the creative subconscious.*
>
> *The **conscious** mind deals with external and internal reality. It perceives, investigates, and interprets information that comes in through the senses....*
>
> *Your **subconscious** handles everything that goes on outside of your consciousness. It's a kind of autopilot that takes care of everything you don't think about—habits, attitudes, and beliefs; many body functions; memories; learned behaviors that have become automatic; feelings that have not been acknowledged or expressed, etc.*
>
> *The **creative subconscious** maintains order by making sure that you behave in ways that reflect your inner version of reality. In other words, it causes you to act like the person you know yourself to be.*

In order to change, grow and develop, we need to get our thinking in order! We need to change some of the "mental tapes" that we have developed over the years. We've heard over and over that human beings have much more potential than they actually use. Ask yourself the following questions:

- Do I have the potential to be a happier person?
- Do I have the potential to be more successful?
- Do I have the potential to make more money?

The answer, typically, would be yes. Well, what is holding you back from using more of your potential? There are many barriers that can get in the way. The focus of my work has been on **attitudes, habits, beliefs and conditioning**. If you want to change, grow, develop or improve, you need to find (and use) some tools and techniques that will help you get past the barriers.

Attitude—*a complex mental state involving beliefs, feelings, values and dispositions to act in certain ways.* As a leader, we need to manage our attitudes. We do not identify them as negative or positive unless and until we set a goal. Is your attitude moving you toward, or away from, your goals? There is no need to change the goal; it is simply a matter of adjusting your attitude!

Habit—*a recurrent, often unconscious, pattern of behavior that is acquired through frequent repetition.* Habits are fine as long as everything stays the same! As a leader, we must be aware that some of our habits will require updating if we expect to grow, change and develop. Changing habits not only takes time, it takes commitment!

Belief—*the mental act, condition or habit of placing trust or confidence in another person or thing.* Beliefs can make or break dreams. Beliefs can make or break teams. What you can accomplish is largely a matter of what you believe! One way to change core beliefs is through the practice of affirmations (which we will cover later in this chapter).

Conditioning—*a process of behavior modification by which a subject comes to associate a desired behavior with a stimulus.* Our upbringing and our conditioning play a key role in who we are, and how we act, as adults. As a leader, we need to be cognizant of this fact and not let it hold us back as we lead the diverse teams that exist in today's workforce.

As I continue to work with senior executives and leaders in my coaching business, I have added to the list of barriers. They include *ego, emotion* and *control*:

Ego—*an inflated feeling of pride in your superiority to others.* As a leader, it is essential to check your ego at the door. This is a conscious act as you reflect on who you are and how you act. One way to get past your ego is by asking people their opinion rather than always telling them the solutions.

Emotion—*a mental state that arises spontaneously rather than through conscious effort and is often accompanied by physiological changes; a feeling.* Emotion is an important attribute in leadership. In the corporate world, it is essential to have a healthy balance between your emotional intelligence and your intellectual intelligence.

Control—*the power to direct or determine.* As a leader, you want to go from control to empowerment. You want to influence your team by providing purpose, direction and inspiration.

Tools for Growth and Change

The reason many people fail in life is that they never really set goals! They have some ideas in mind of what they would like to do, what they would like to change, what they would like to try. But it usually stops there. Setting goals, and achieving them, takes work, effort and energy. And, most importantly, it takes commitment.

The following are five effective tools to personal development and growth:

#1—Self-talk

The paramount tool for effective professional and personal development is self-talk. That inner dialogue that goes on, all day long, can either move us toward or away from our goals. Worry is negative goal setting. Control your self-talk to be positive, forward thinking and uplifting. Know that in some ways negative self-talk is a habit and we have become very good at it! With a little focus and diligence, habits can be changed.

> » My son is a high school teacher and he has developed the habit of going for long walks over the lunch hour. When I asked him why he did this, rather than join his senior colleagues (from whom he could learn

and grow) for lunch, he replied that the negative self-talk in that room was too depressing for him. **«**

Teams can have negative self-talk, as can organizations. A leader needs to be very aware of their vocabulary and how they speak to people. Know that how you speak is a direct reflection of the way you think!

The following is an example from a client of how one leader reduces negativity in the workplace:

> **»** One day, it suddenly became clear to me how contagious group negativity is. When noticing heightened negativity, I would send an email to my team advising that "today is elastic day." This powerful self-awareness exercise of wearing an elastic band on our wrists for a day reminded them to be mindful of negativity. And it works! **«**

To help build your self-awareness about your negative thinking, consider a time when you wanted to try something new, or were deciding whether to apply for a promotion or a new job. The following four questions can help you identify your self-talk regarding this event:

- Did your self-talk initially stop you from applying for a promotion?
- Did you doubt yourself or think negatively about the interview process?
- What specific self-talk could you have changed to support rather than doubt yourself?
- What good advice would you give to a friend in a similar situation?

#2—Life Balance Wheel

Have you ever driven in a car with a flat tire? Are you going through your work and personal life feeling much the same way? It is more important than ever these days, especially as a woman in a leadership role, to learn how to maintain balance in your life. The life balance wheel is a fundamental tool, for both personal and professional growth. (You can google "life balance wheel" and find many different samples of this tool on the Internet for your use.) Complete the balance wheel twice a year and use it to identify some specific areas of your life (and career) for development and improvement. Typically, I would focus on no more than three areas (for example, physical health, recreation and finances) and set goals accordingly. From this, you can set goals for change. As a leader, the balance wheel can be easily customized to a business setting and the individual spokes labeled as different competencies. It is a very effective way to help people understand and embrace areas for change.

#3—Goal Setting

Goal setting works! Knowing what you want in life and writing it down makes it real and elevates your level of commitment to the outcome. Not writing down your goals is actually a form of self-sabotage. As a leader, it is essential that you establish clear and exciting goals for your own development, and to inspire your team accordingly. The exercise that follows can help you do that:

1. Use the balance wheel and customize it to a workplace environment. Label the spokes accordingly—for example, Sales, Marketing, Professional Development, Human Resources, Financial, Communication…

2. Once you have completed the balance wheel, identify three areas for improvement.

3. For each of those three areas, write a vision statement to describe what you want that competency to "look like and feel like" in 12 months.

4. From each of the vision statements, work backwards to identify, specifically, what action steps are required to reach the vision.

5. Once you have identified five to seven action steps (these became the goals), prioritize them, date them, and review these steps weekly.

This exercise will help you to identify new goals (strategically and consistently) and to monitor your progress. It is essential that you celebrate your success along the way! This helps to build internal efficacy.

#4—Vision Board

**To become a great leader, you need to have a vision
and you need to communicate that vision.**

This is one of the most effective tools I have used in the last 15 years, both in my teaching and coaching with others and for myself. It's simply a matter of taking your goals and transferring them to bristol board by using pictures. We know how the mind works—pictures are extremely effective when it comes to imprinting images on the brain. (Look at the power of advertising!)

Find pictures that match your goals and stick them to a bright piece of bristol board. Place the board somewhere that you can see it numerous times in a day. Add words/phrases that support your goals as well. As leaders, we work with our teams to create a vision for the future. There is no more powerful tool than taking the company's vision statement and, working together, creating a vision board for the next one, five or ten years. In this way, each person gets to add a picture to the board and "owns" the vision. As a leader, it is our role to continuously communicate the vision—this board can be revisited at meetings throughout the year. As human beings, we move toward what we think about!

> *Get a mental picture of what you want every aspect of your life to be like in 5, 10, 15, and 20 years from now and write it down. Read and adjust it every few weeks; it will happen. We get what we want. Have a clear picture!*
>
> Randie J., owner/operator, home improvement field

#5—Affirmation Writing

Affirmations are the tool that brings it all together. Having a goal, writing it down, visualizing the end result—and writing affirmations—is the perfect, little package. Affirmations are written statements that imprint a message on the creative subconscious, causing you to move forward with intent and energy to achieve your goals. There are a few guidelines for writing effective affirmations. They are:

- Write affirmations in the first person, present tense;
- Use positive words when writing affirmations (write what you DO want, not what you DO NOT want);
- Keep your affirmation statements brief, clear and succinct;
- Write affirmation statements that are specific;
- Ensure your affirmation statements are realistic;
- Affirmations need to be written by the person that they are for—meaning yourself;

- Ensure your affirmation statements are sincere (linked to your goals).

Write your affirmation statements on 3 x 5 inch (colored) index cards and carry them with you. You will want to begin with only five to eight affirmations and read them daily. Then increase the number of times a day you read them. When you take baby steps with a new habit, you are more likely to stick with it and achieve success.

As a leader, it is powerful and effective to develop individual and team affirmations. These affirmations can be displayed in meeting rooms, individual offices and lunch rooms, for example. They can help you to move forward with collective energy and drive to achieve great success and measurable outcomes.

Putting It All Together

Let's look at how these five tools for growth and change—self-talk, life balance wheel, goal setting, vision boards, and affirmations—work together for goal attainment. The following personal example began with a dream:

> » I saw the brochure for a world tour of the northern hemisphere on a private plane. My imagination began to run wild. What an incredible journey that would be! Eight of the ten places on the tour were on my own "dream travel list." What would it be like to take this trip?
>
> Then, my **self-talk** kicked in... thinking that it was only "rich" people who took these kinds of trips. Where will you ever get the money for this kind of adventure? Being an entrepreneur and self-employed, how can I be away for a full month? My self-defeating thoughts won out—for the moment.
>
> That brochure sat on my desk and I looked at it in the following weeks. Images of the plane, the globe and the destinations were becoming firmly imprinted in my brain (**the vision**).
>
> Problem solving began. I set the goal of taking some of the profit from the sale of my house and using it for this incredible trip (**the goal**). Next, I taped travel pictures (including one of myself) to a large, bright piece of bristol board (**the vision board**). Consciously, I began to change my self-talk (the inner dialogue) and tell myself that I deserved to go on

that trip, that the finances would be managed, and that I could even make it a "working vacation"! To change my self-talk, I began writing **affirmations** and reading them to myself three, four, five, six…sometimes ten times a day, each day. This began to change the internal picture of my reality. These affirmations included:

- My income is constantly increasing.
- Today, I speak up for myself and ask (the universe) for what I want.
- I am prosperous, well, and on my way around the world.

To make a long story short, I went on the trip. And I'm going again with all expenses paid this time—which is a testament to the application of these concepts in my personal life. **«**

Professional Development

- What career goals, dreams or aspirations do you have?
- What core beliefs are holding you back from succeeding in your career?
- What habits have you developed that require change for you to be seen as a positive leader?
- Is your ego in check?

Success is often about common sense. Though not taught in school, young leaders need to learn some common sense basics supported by tools for application. As well, they need strong mentors to coach and guide them as they advance in their careers. With that in mind, the following are the seven top core competencies you need to develop in order to succeed in business today.

1. Critical Thinking Skills

> *A former U.S. Secretary of Labor was asked where he would spend federal funds if he had just one shot at improving America's labor force. His reply was simple: "Thinking skills."*
>
> Guy Hale

Helping staff to develop critical thinking skills means that current business plans, policies and procedures are likely to be challenged. If this challenge is accepted and valued within an environment that encourages continuous learning, it can only lead to improved business practice and an increase in the bottom line. Critical thinking skills include problem solving, decision making, goal setting, positive attitude, motivation, and so on.

> *People hire people on attitude. A good supervisor will let*
> *you implement your new ideas, because when trying*
> *different things you gain experience.*
> Terry D., director of a post-secondary institute

2. Communication Skills

One of the greatest challenges in corporations today is having four generations in the workplace. And for women leaders, each generation has their own biases and experiences that impact your working relationship. Communication skills, and values about same, are as diverse as the clothes we wear! In this age of technology, it is increasingly common to find individuals:

- Hiding behind email when communication should be in person;
- Addicted to their communication devices, using cell phones and/or the BlackBerry when they are actually in meetings with people;
- Responding to emails at all times of the day (and expecting immediate responses).

Dare to be different—make it a point to communicate face-to-face with individuals at every possible opportunity. The benefits far outweigh the convenience of technology. As a leader, your people do not care what you know, but they do want to know that you care!

3. Integrity and Ethical Behavior

"You can't go wrong when you do what is right!" I often said that to myself when it was time, as a leader, to make some of the tough decisions. As a coach and a mentor, it is my constant recommendation to new leaders.

*Develop and maintain your **integrity** no matter what. You have complete control over it. To live with no regrets is priceless and enduring; to live without a BMW or the corner office, is not that big of a deal. Better a little with integrity than a lot you have to give back later.*

Steve B., Royal Canadian Mounted Police (RCMP)

Tip: Always keep your promises! Tell the truth! It's as simple as that.

4. Building Trust

Building trust is enormously powerful in an organization. People will not do their best without it. Warren Bennis (founding chairman of the Leadership Institute at the University of Southern California) calls it the major leadership challenge of today and tomorrow. Trust promotes teamwork, open communication and sharing. A culture of trust is a valuable asset for leaders who are able to develop it, and maintain it. How can you build trust in an organization? Ensure that your word is gold! And adopt my favorite philosophy: "If it is to be, it's up to me!"

Tip: Some of the top ways to build trust in your team include:
- Acting and speaking consistently;
- Sharing information;
- Doing what's right;
- Keeping an open mind!

5. Working as a Team

It is good to be individually smart, strong and efficacious. But your performance will rarely exceed expectations unless you are able to work in a team and harness each other's talents and expertise. Companies emphasize teamwork and the sharing of knowledge over hierarchy and titles. As a leader, you need to make everyone on your team a goal setter; let everyone be creative and innovative. Women leaders know how to build self-esteem in individuals, which in the long run helps to strengthen the team.

Tip: Set a goal to reward individuals for their contributions on a regular basis. Remember to praise in public and criticize in private. Third-party affirmation of your team members is a powerful way to build and strengthen the team.

6. Networking

Business is based on relationships. It's not what you know, but who you know. Develop some strong networking strategies and practices. Ensure that you have identified the value in attending certain events (is there a match with your particular career goals?), do your homework in advance, and be prepared once you arrive. Not every business event is worth your time and effort. And not every networking opportunity is a business event! Some questions to ask yourself in advance are:

1. Do you have enough business cards (and take them with you!)? You might be surprised at how many people attend networking events and do not have a business card with them.
2. Who attends these events? Who do you specifically want to meet?
3. How will you meet, greet and listen to people?
4. What networking questions have you prepared?
5. How do you exit a conversation strategically, and move on?
6. How do you manage food, beverage and conversation all at once?

Networking is a learned skill. As an aspiring leader, find a mentor who has mastered this skill and attend some networking events with him or her. Watch them in action. As a leader, it's all about your network! Developing and maintaining relationships is worth its weight in gold.

7. Public Speaking

This is said to be the thing people fear most—even more than death! As an aspiring leader, it is important to practice and perfect your public speaking skills. Whether this applies to a situation where you are making introductions around a boardroom table or a major presentation in front of colleagues or shareholders, it is an essential leadership skill. Join a Toastmasters group or a Christopher Leadership course, and then seize every opportunity to practice those skills.

Tip: When required to give presentations, the more intimate and confident you are with your subject matter, the easier it is to speak about it. All that remains is to handle the environmental details (using a microphone, room set-up, etc.). Improve your skills at every opportunity, and regularly ask for feedback. Read *Feel the Fear and Do It Anyway* by Susan Jeffers. Leaders with strong public speaking skills exude confidence and gain attention. Mastering this skill will elevate you in the ranks!

Does This Really Apply in the Workforce?

Following up with some of the young women who participated in the first Leadership Institute program, I asked them about their learning and what was real and sustainable in their current careers. Here are their comments:

Dawn: Network, network, network.

Annette: Invest in yourself and your future! Don't expect someone else to do it for you.

Robin: Public speaking skills are essential. Get past your fears and perfect your skills.

> *Have passion for whatever you do. If you ever lose the*
> *passion, be brave and find something else to do.*
>
> Kate A., hospitality industry

Top 10 Steps for Strong Women Leaders

For the past many years, I have experienced significant changes in my life, both personally and professionally. The leadership competencies and skills outlined in this chapter have helped me to be flexible, resilient, creative and successful. I have worked at all levels, in many sectors, including as a board member and volunteer in the non-profit sector. I have been able to create a "cheat sheet" for becoming a better me!

The following are 10 steps you can take right now to become an authentic, effective and progressive leader:

1.   Learn the art of self-awareness;
2.   Develop a strong vision for your life, and write it down;

3. Control your self-talk to be positive and uplifting, and practice this daily;

4. Stretch your comfort zone and take risks;

5. Ask for what you want, knowing that "if it is to be, it's up to me!"

6. Develop habits to ensure balance in your life;

7. Lighten up—this is not a dress rehearsal;

8. Take action to develop and maintain relationships with great mentors;

9. Put your life and your work on a "want to, choose to, like it, love it" basis;

10. If you aren't happy with who you are and what you do, then change it.

Become the best "you" that you can be. Believe in yourself in your role!

Pat Mussieux

As a professional speaker, **Pat Mussieux** has designed and presented programs to major universities, conferences, corporate workshops, retreats and professional associations. Her specialty is in the area of personal accountability and goal setting. She has become an expert at making big dreams become reality!

As a volunteer, Pat has dedicated over 25 years of service to organizations, such as Centre High and the Edmonton Prison for Women, in a mentoring capacity, and the United Way and the Alzheimer Society. She was instrumental in leading the five-year initiative to reorganize the Alzheimer Society on a provincial level in Alberta, Canada, as they moved toward "One Vision, One Society, One Voice."

Pat is the author of *Who Am I Now? Simple Steps to Inventing Your Future After Divorce, Retirement, Death of a Spouse, Empty Nest...* Her second book, *Where Am I Now? The Story of My Tour Around the World in a Private Plane*, will be released in fall 2007.

Business Name: Purple People Leaders
Address: 107 Duchess Avenue
                   London, ON N6C 1N7
Telephone: 519.433.4939
Email: pat@patmussieux.com
Web address: www.patmussieux.com

Favorite Quote:
If it is to be, it's up to me!

Do not go where the path may lead, go instead where there is no path and leave a trail.

Ralph Waldo Emerson

Diane King

Group Intersol, Diane King Inc.

Quiet Leaders Among Us

You don't have to be a "person of influence" to be influential.
In fact, the most influential people in my life are probably not
even aware of the things they've taught me.

Scott Adams

Quiet leaders don't have to move mountains, bring businesses to greatness or rise to lofty political heights. Quiet leaders are content with making a positive difference, whether it's in their family, their community, or their work.

The words "quiet leader" first came to me when I was writing a eulogy for my maternal grandmother in 1990. She was my role model and a light in my life. When I tried to find a word for her, the only thing that kept coming up was "quiet leader." Now, this was a woman who didn't work outside the home, she didn't raise money in her community, she didn't travel in high social circles. No, she was just a rural woman who raised eight children really well. Her legacy is that her children, spread out over Québec and New England, still get together six to eight times a year and talk to each other over the phone frequently.

» At her wake my grandmother's 19 grandchildren remembered her as someone who made each of us feel special. (We all thought we were her favorite!) We remembered her words of wisdom—words that have influenced decisions in my life as well as influenced the things I tell my own children. Her pearls of wisdom include: "soyez toujours fiers" (be proud of who you are), "un éducation n'est jamais perdu" (an education is never lost), and most important, "deux langues c'est deux personnes" (having two languages is like being two people). **«**

All of the grandchildren strive to be the best that we can be, the majority of us are bilingual and all have post-secondary education. And it is extending to our own children. My grandmother may not have thought that she was affecting the world, or even her little community, but her influence on her family is having a far-reaching and positive effect on the world today. She was a quiet leader.

Big "L" Leaders

Society has always valued and emphasized big "L" leadership. Of course we have had great leaders in our times: Martin Luther King Jr., John F. Kennedy, Pierre Trudeau, and Winston Churchill, to name a few. They all shared the same characteristics of great vision, passion, and hard work, and were able to "rally the troops." They led through very difficult times. These big "L" leaders are often used as examples of what to strive for.

We also have examples of great leaders in organizations: people with great vision and the courage to make changes for the good of the organization, for example, Lee Iacocca at Chrysler, Jan Carlzon at Scandinavian Airlines System, and Bill Gates at Microsoft. So, as bottom lines have improved and businesses reap more profits, the characteristics of these leaders have been held up as the Holy Grail of Leadership. But is leadership only about the big "L" leader?

A few years ago an intriguing article, "Level 5 Leadership," written by Jim Collins, appeared in the *Harvard Business Review* (www.hbr.org). Collins sparked my curiosity when he stated that most leaders only make it up to level 4 leadership, which he calls the "effective leader." Of the 1435 companies they researched for this study, 1424 made it to level 4. That left only 11 companies with level 5 leaders! Interestingly, many of the names of the level 4 leaders were recognizable. Not so with the names of the level 5 leaders. The level 4 leaders had the typical traits that we associate with strong leaders: visionary, determined, purposeful. So, what was it that made level 5 leaders so special?

It was actually very simple and very powerful. It was the combination of humility and will: a strong determination to do the right thing, coupled with modesty. And this describes quiet leaders. I'm sure you can think of people you've met within organizations who have these traits. So, who are these quiet leaders?

Quiet Leaders Among Us

Quiet leaders are the lifeline of our families, our communities, and our organizations. They are the ones who ensure that things get done, they take initiative, they live their lives with passion, they care about others, they listen, they take care of themselves. They are genuine. They know their values and they live them…and they do it with little fanfare. This does not mean that they're shy or withdrawn. It's just that they don't call unnecessary attention to themselves.

Quiet leaders are that way simply by being who they are.

You probably recall people in your life who have had a positive impact either on yourself or others around you. These are the people who I consider quiet leaders. Some might be in a position of authority, such as a school teacher, manager, or business owner, but many are just ordinary people doing extraordinary things in their own quiet way. What makes them special is that they aren't trying to be special.

When identifying the characteristics of quiet leaders, the same traits kept coming up time and time again.

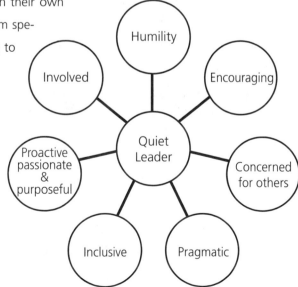

The reality is that big "L" leaders are but a tip of the iceberg; they are the *visible* 10 percent. What's beneath the surface are the strong, determined, and modest quiet leaders who are really holding our society together. For without our quiet leaders—in our families, in our community, and in our work—people's brilliance and greatness would not shine through. A colleague, Judith, shared the following with me:

» The quiet leaders that come to mind are the people that were often called on to oversee a difficult project, or an interdepartmental group whose members might not all be on the same page, because they were known to be able to manage any conflict. But they didn't take charge in an aggressive way, weren't flamboyant, and didn't create or exacerbate crisis attitudes; they quietly and effectively pulled people together and got the job done.

I think a key characteristic of these people is "quiet"—they listen more than talk. And because they listen well, everyone in the group feels heard, and co-operation typically ensues. Maybe people within the group have some conflict, but this person is a common denominator that everyone can rely on to consider his/her points of view.

There's a high level of trust that builds for this type of leader so that even if some within the group don't get their way, they can usually accept the result as being fair because the leader listened, considered, and communicated effectively. «

Judith may be referring to her work environment, but her words also reflect the stories that surfaced about the quiet leaders all around us, in ordinary situations at home and at work. They live, work, and play among us. Sometimes we recognize them. More often we don't because it's easy to take them for granted. But make no mistake, when things are going really well, it's usually because there is a quiet leader nearby who—by virtue of just being who they are and doing what they do naturally—ensures that things go smoothly.

So, the question is, are you a quiet leader who isn't recognizing the positive difference that you make? The following are some of the key qualities and traits of quiet leaders.

#1—Quiet Leaders Are Encouraging

Quiet leaders often focus on the growth of others, whether it's in the family, community or at work. They see the potential in others and help them to develop it. There are countless stories of people taking a young person under their wing and offering him, or her, a chance at education, redemption, a career…it's someone who can see the spark in another and flame the ember so it glows. My friend, Marie, relates the following:

> » One of my past dance teachers was a woman who was able to inspire me to pursue my desire to better myself; I think she had the ability to make a quiet difference in many people's lives. She had the uncanny ability to see people's potential and could empower them to translate intention into reality. She would inspire you to take on a new challenge; she would make you feel safe, loved, and self-confident. I'm not quite sure how she did it, but I remember feeling amazed at how she was able to make everyone feel unique and special.
>
> She could focus on me as if no one else was there, and somehow reach in, deep inside of me, to awaken my creative desires. I believe that she nourished herself by helping others progress and I remember how she would ask me to connect with those who had similar passions so that we could exchange value and help each other. Ingrid's life was eventually taken away by incurable cancer, and after her death I remember talking to others about her. It quickly became obvious that she had had the same effect on them. «

Self-Assessment

- Are you more inward focused (on yourself) or more outward focused (on others)?
- Do you take a special interest in what others are interested in?
- Do you give others encouragement that is individualized?
- Do you look for and recognize the potential in others?

#2—Quiet Leaders Are Involved

Quiet leaders are no strangers to jumping in with both feet. They lead through their exuberance, their joy, and their example. Others are swept up in the moment and want to be around the quiet leader. One of my clients, Marc, tells this story:

>> My fondest memory is of my elementary school principal. He was a very friendly man. He always had a smile, no matter where anyone would run into him. Finding warmth from adults in a world that can be so frightening was always a source of security for a child.

Mr. Fraser always partook in all of the activities of the school. If there was a "Jump Rope for Heart" fundraiser, he'd be there in the school brand jogging suit. (It was red and white at the time.) During school liturgies at our church next door, he was often at the front of the gathering with his guitar. He led us all in song with unrestrained enthusiasm. All 600 students from kindergarten to grade six would sing in unison. I have never felt such joy in all my life as I did when that church was full of song. Mr. Fraser was a part of that. <<

Self-Assessment
* Do you get involved in activities at work, in your community, or in your family? How do you get involved?
* Are you openly enthusiastic?
* Do people love being in your company?

#3—Quiet Leaders Are Proactive, Passionate, and Purposeful

Quiet leaders see what needs to be done...and take the initiative to get it done. They either do things themselves in a quiet way or they mobilize others because their passion is infectious. They aren't leaders because they're telling others what to do; they're leading by rolling up their sleeves and just doing it. Heather offers the following example of a quiet leader in action:

>> Jim was an Area Commissioner for Scouts a couple of years ago. He

took the job and really made it his own. He organized training sessions for leaders within his area, went to meetings, and took on a personal challenge. His goal was to save the training area nearby from being closed permanently. He researched, wrote to the bigwigs in Toronto, developed a five-year business plan to keep the place functioning, and organized a meeting at the camp for the bigwigs with all the leaders and the Scouts, Cubs, and Beavers in attendance. His quiet determination and leadership saved a valuable commodity for the children to be able to use at no cost for camping, training, and day hiking.

There are many more examples I could give you of other times I've witnessed him in action over the 10 years he was an active Scouting member, as well as at work.

Hope this helps...don't tell Jim, he'd be embarrassed that I told you. He makes me so proud...his influence and example through Scouting, and as a father, have allowed us to enjoy the results in our son; his mannerisms, his pride, his sensitivity and understanding of others...he follows in Jim's footsteps. **«**

Self-Assessment

- Do you feel strongly about things being right in the world?
- Do you take the initiative to get things rolling?
- Are you focused on the goals?
- Are you passionate about it?

#4—Quiet Leaders Have Concern for Others

Quiet leaders are fair and have a genuine concern for others. They want to make a positive difference in other people's lives and will often put others before themselves. This is not about martyrdom, but rather about a true joy in helping others get what they need or want.

In the workplace it might be the manager who unselfishly helps an employee to grow and move beyond their current role, even if it means losing them from their team. There are managers who prefer to stifle a good employee's growth, preventing them from moving ahead, for fear of losing them. That is the antithesis of a quiet leader. A quiet leader revels in the growth and of being able to see someone "spread their wings." Laurie's story exemplifies the quiet leader in a position of authority:

» One of the quiet leaders I am blessed to know is my boss. She has the skills, knowledge, talent, and experience to serve at senior management levels but made the conscious choice to remain as a middle manager (director level) because it positioned her better to influence within the organization.

She has an incredible reputation in our organization for being honest and pushing people to achieve their best. People know that while they may not always like what she has to say, she speaks from the heart and always in their best interests. On a personal level, she has guided me in my development and advised me based on what I needed and what would advance me, rather than only taking organizational needs into consideration. «

Self-Assessment

- Do you help others grow, even if it means them moving beyond you?
- Do you cheer others' successes?
- Do you have others' best interests at heart?

#5—Quiet Leaders Foster Inclusiveness

Quiet leaders see the good in others. They strive to make the world a better place by fostering understanding, acceptance, and love of others. They exemplify their values by how they live and work. Lise shares the following story:

» Frère Artur Gravelle taught social studies at my high school. He could best be described as an avant-garde teacher who was passionate about life, laughter, and learning.

Always in a happy mood and open to human interaction, this man exemplified wisdom and understanding. He valued people from all walks of life and taught us to love one another, regardless of race, religion, or culture differences. He promoted open dialogue on every, and any, subject matter, and taught his students to respect their many differences, even if they did not agree with what was said or put forth. Frère Artur taught us to love our fellow man and to put their needs ahead of our own, even if at times the cost was detrimental to us on a personal level.

The quality that I most cherished in Frère Artur was his ability to make you feel special whenever you came into contact with him. He always had a smile and a kind word and he spread his *joie de vivre* generously. **

Self-Assessment

- Do you share your joy openly?
- Do you see the good in people?
- Are you the one who brings people together?

#6—Quiet Leaders Are Pragmatic

Quiet leaders are realistic optimists. They don't see the world through rose-colored glasses, but neither do they focus on the negative. Their motto is, "If the world hands you lemons, make lemonade!"

» About a year ago, my mother-in-law was diagnosed with stage-three lung cancer. A feisty Cornish woman from the Southwest of England, she raised two boys while working shifts as a nurse. How she's handling the disease and her eventual passing is courageous and inspiring.

She's taken a very practical approach to her treatments. She's very straightforward with what's going on. She is her own best advocate and insists on treatments even when doctors have seemed to give up on her. And she talks openly about everything with her family. She jokes about her ashes being put on our mantles, or having them scattered in our gardens. She makes it easy for us to discuss these things openly with her.

She's sold her house of 45 years and, despite living day-to-day, she's moving into a condominium! It's been her dream, since before she got sick, to move into a condo near all her friends. She wasn't about to let a little illness stop her from achieving that. In spite of failing health, she took on this great task. This doesn't mean she's in denial, but rather that she refused the option of putting her dream on hold to lie about the house waiting to die. She decided to *live* with cancer.

Watching someone go through a battle with cancer is very stressful, but the experience has been made less so because of my mother-in-law's attitude toward life. She's helping herself and her family go through this in a practical, realistic, and calm way. I appreciate and admire her for that.

When I think of situations where I might be stuck for a way of handling things, I find myself increasingly thinking, "How would Barb handle this?" and I find myself coming up with just the right answer. She gives me guidance without even knowing it...and I'm sure she will long after she's gone. **«**

Self-Assessment

- Do you see the practical side of things?
- Are you unafraid to deal with difficult subjects?
- Do you take on challenges well?

#7—Quiet Leaders Are Humble

> *Fail to honor people, They will fail to honor you;*
> *But of a good leader, who talks little,*
> *When his work is done, his aim fulfilled,*
> *They will all say, "We did this ourselves."*
>
> Lao-Tzu

Quiet leaders don't seek the attention they sometimes get. They appreciate sincere thanks but are usually surprised and/or embarrassed by public accolades and are often giving credit to others around them. They do what they do because they love it, see a need, and feel that anyone would do the same in their shoes. They usually see themselves as just "normal" people.

» Diane traveled around the world, with her family, for four years, chronicling their adventures in the local newspaper every Saturday. She wrote

Leadership Gurus Speak Out!

about the people they met and the situations in which they found themselves. Over time, Diane developed a following of very devoted readers. As the family's travels took them to the world's poorest countries, the tone of the articles changed and it became evident that the poverty, coupled with the immense generosity of the people they met, changed Diane and her family. They became much more aware of the problems in the world and needed to find a way to help.

Through her articles, people were inspired to donate to the various causes that the family came upon. On their return, Diane started a small kitchen-table charity that raises money to send youth to school and to renovate schools in disrepair in Kenya. Through this, she became a reluctant celebrity. This bothered her as people began to treat her differently. She didn't see herself as special; it was the donors who were making a difference.

It was her humility that galvanized people to action and allowed the charity to flourish. Her favorite saying was, "One pebble, plinking down a mountainside, can start an avalanche." She truly believed that one small act could make a big difference in the world and the donors were doing just that. **«**

Self-Assessment

- Do you give credit to others before accepting it for yourself?
- Are you uncomfortable with public recognition focused just on you?
- Do you find yourself often deflecting accolades away from you and towards others who have helped in a project?

Quiet Leaders—Made or Born?

Quiet leaders seem to come into this world with the seeds of these leadership qualities inside of them. For some, these qualities are so strong that their brilliance shines through and they develop into quiet leaders on their own, sometimes without realizing the positive impact that they have on others. These are the quiet, confident leaders who are comfortable being themselves.

Others are the quiet leaders-in-waiting. They're the ones who have the seed in them but have been socialized or persuaded by society, school, or work to be someone they aren't. They have bought into the paradigms of the big "L" leaders and either work hard at being like that (and are usually uncomfortable doing it) or they give up ever thinking they can make a difference.

For quiet leaders-in-waiting, the right conditions can lead to a shift in perspective, allowing their brilliance to shine through. Self-reflection, or a profoundly transformative life event, can also lead to someone becoming more comfortable with who they really are. Anne-Marie shared the following story:

» When I was 16, I attended a youth leadership camp. It was a very intense experience for me as I seemed to be quieter than the others and wondered what I was doing there. The others were all striving to show off their leadership abilities and I was more than happy to stay in the background and let them take their place.

One day we did an activity in silence, or at least as much silence as some of these people could muster. We had to figure out a solution to a maze and get people in the right places. There was much confusion and commotion: arms flailing, grimaces, and grunts as people tried to tell each other what to do—in silence! I saw the solution fairly quickly and was amazed that no one seemed to be getting it. There was lots of action, but no results.

I waited and waited for someone to come up with the answer, sure that one of these strong leaders would see it soon enough. Finally, I couldn't stand it anymore and I raised both my arms and made signals for people to look at me. I outlined the solution and got people moving in the right direction. I got them out of the chaos!

In the debriefing afterwards, the facilitator confirmed that I had had the solution fairly early and asked why I hadn't said anything. That's when I realized that I wasn't comfortable taking the lead on things and usually stayed in the background. That exercise made me realize that just because there are people who are busy being leaders, it doesn't mean they actually know what they're doing. It made me value my own intelligence, intuition, and abilities. It was a turning point for me—in my confidence level—for I realized that leadership was not simply about doing a lot of things. It was about being there, quietly observing, trusting myself, and having the confidence to step in when needed. I've since been very comfortable with my leadership abilities, knowing that I can just be a leader by trusting myself and being me. I'm lucky, I learned that at 16. **«**

Are You a Quiet Leader?

Society seems to put such an emphasis on the big "L" leaders, and the things that they accomplish, that it's easy to overlook the value and importance of the quiet leaders. People who go about their lives making a difference often have an attitude of "that's just me." They think they are not doing anything "special"; they're not even necessarily aware of the ripple effect of their actions. I'm sure that the quiet leaders in the preceding stories were aware of the results of the things they did, but were they aware of the unseen differences they made in people's lives? The feelings of hope, confidence, and joy that they engendered just by being who they are—the role models that they are to others. Quiet leaders, ironically, aren't often privy to the real difference that they make. It's about touching someone—in their heart and in their soul.

So, are you a quiet leader or a quiet leader-in-waiting? How do you choose to live your life? A good friend once said, "To the world, you might be one person but to one person, you might be the world."

Being a quiet leader is being that one person.

Diane King

Diane King is a bilingual facilitator, coach, and consultant, whose main passion is working with intact teams, helping people work better together through more effective interpersonal relations. Her approach is practical, collaborative, and is inspired by an unquenchable desire to bring out the best in her clients. Diane is a playful inspirer of teams, whose insatiable curiosity helps members and their leaders discover their own brilliance.

In addition to numerous professional development courses, Diane holds her Masters in Human Systems Intervention (Organization Development) from Concordia University and her BA (Social Communications) from the University of Ottawa. She is a neuro-linguistic programming (NLP) practitioner and has her Advanced Mediation Certificate (University of Windsor).

Diane has also co-authored two books: *Achieve It! A Personal Success Journal* (ISBN 0-9699941-0-9) and *The Standard Clause Handbook* for the real estate industry in Halifax.

Business Name: Group Intersol, Diane King Inc.
Address: 211 des Fondateurs, Gatineau, QC J9J 1M4
Telephone: 819-682-6021 or 613-230-6424
Email: dking@intersol.ca
Web Address: www.intersol.ca
Professional Affiliations: International Association of Facilitators; Organization
                         Development Network of Ottawa/Outaouais

Favorite Quote:
*Heaven's not a place that you go when you die. It's that
moment in life when you actually feel alive!*
                         From the song "The Tide" by Spill Canvas

Peter M. Cleveland

Cleveland Leadership Group Inc.

Anatomy of Accountability

So much has been written in recent years on the subject of accountability. WorldCom, Enron, government, and other financial scandals have caused regulators to re-examine accountability effectiveness to stakeholders. However, little has been written about what it really means to be accountable. What makes some people accountable while others are not? What affects our ability to be accountable? Without knowing the answers to these questions, we cannot even begin to understand personal or organizational accountability.

It's Accountability, Not Governance!

Some experts will have you believe governance creates accountability; others believe more rules will result in more accountability success. Yet, nothing can be further from the truth! You cannot legislate accountability. We are not that adaptable. You cannot make people do the right thing at the right time with more rules. More rules just penalize those who are already accountable, while creating nothing more than temporary roadblocks for those who are not. Unaccountable people will always find ways to take shortcuts, work around rules for their own benefit, or barely satisfy their job description. So if we want to truly understand accountability we must understand its anatomy. Only with a clear understanding of what creates a sense of accountability in each of us is it possible to understand organizational accountability. Let's explore.

Accountability, for the most part, is demonstrated when people are relied on to achieve agreed upon goals, objectives and outcomes—to do what they say they will do when they said they will do it. It is demonstrated when organizations are relied on to meet expectations of customers, shareholders, employees, legislators and regulators. And, accountable work environments exist when people rely on each other to keep performance commitments and agreements. If "he's a man of his word," he takes action consistent with his professional and personal goals. If others rely on you and you feel a strong sense of reliance on yourself and those around you, you have the fundamental basis to build accountability.

Accountability emerges from personal behavior and is driven by a developed sense of values arising from personality and childhood development, education, environment, level of happiness, and station in life. These forces shape how we react to opportunities, challenges and threats—whether we honestly see the situation as it really is or as we would like it to be—whether we are honest with ourselves and others.

Such forces help develop, create and reinforce our personal rules or, what we call in computer language, the motherboard of our personal operating system—the sense of values and priorities we use to make decisions. It determines how we evaluate alternate courses of action, make decisions and maintain accountability as a foundational value in life.

Personal operating systems are the lens through which we view life, business, and the way we conduct ourselves—all we do in the name of personal beliefs. It determines whether we take responsibility for our actions rather than pass blame to others. It is about having the character to speak out against wrong when you may be criticized. It's challenging ideas that you know will fail, no matter how unpopular you become. It is about having ethics, to know right from wrong, to see black and white, and to have a process to deal with all that is grey. And, it is about having the will and courage to answer and be answerable. The determination to be both consistent with, and faithful to, values such as honesty and integrity, and to be 100 percent responsible for goals, separates those who are accountable from those who are not.

Many people talk about accountability, fewer live it. Some feel they are above accountability; a perception we often have of politicians. Many trumpet the values of accountability, and then avoid it with every move. Many believe in it as long as it doesn't affect them: "John should be held accountable for the failure of that product. I was only on the review team. I didn't invent the damn thing."

What Makes Organizations Accountable?

Employers have different degrees of accountability, that is, the level their corporate culture permits. Some encourage it at every turn, while others just pay lip service to it. Organizations positively affect personal accountability when they talk regularly about:

Trust, integrity, honor:
- Encouraging a culture of rising above one's current responsibilities to contribute to vision achievement;
- Not tolerating conflicts of interest;
- Ensuring freedom and protection to communicate wrongdoing ("whistle-blowers");
- Accepting representations based only upon facts;
- Discouraging fear around full, complete and truthful communication;
- Respecting others and their opinions;
- Avoiding organizational politics and game playing;
- Making commitments and living up to them.

Transparency and ethics:
- Leadership that communicates on all matters openly and often;
- Everyone stands up to admit mistakes;
- Advising the organization of internal wrongdoing and conflicts of interest;
- Never entering a transaction, discussion or communication with any stakeholder that is less than legal, honest, fair and above reproach.

Linkage of corporate vision to daily behavior:
- Leadership that involves everyone in goal achievement;
- Leadership that clearly and frequently communicates goals, policies and procedures necessary for every organization level to contribute to vision achievement;

- Board of directors has a policy to disclose errors.
- The ability to accept constructive criticism and to focus all energy toward continuous improvement;
- Asking for education and knowledge to improve your contribution to corporate goal achievement.

Organizational structure built upon stakeholder needs:
- The ability to anticipate the needs of stakeholders and take action to meet those needs before being asked to do so;
- Constantly pursuing new and better ways to service stakeholders.

Regularly communicating these policies and rewarding those who follow them daily, while at the same time delivering exceptional stakeholder care, builds and maintains cultures of accountability. More exposure to positively reinforced cultures draws out accountable behavior—employees become accountability-drawn. Conversely, leading and managing an organization based upon fear if rules are broken creates an environment of:
- Distrust;
- Encouraging silence for fear of reprisal;
- Doing nothing more than the minimum standard of care;
- Giving nothing more that the strict definition of your responsibilities;
- Not risking help to others;
- Not understanding the impact of your daily activity on vision achievement.

Organizations with these cultures try to force accountability through rules and penalties. Because they try to push accountability, they become accountability-pushed organizations. At best their success is mediocre; at worst they fail.

The cost of poor accountability is enormous and stems from eight primary areas:

1. Poor stakeholder care: Customers and, hence, sales are lost because of poor care—a real and measurable cost. Poor service, unreliable products, or a lack of enduring relationships drive customers in the direction of competitors. Regulatory agencies may spend more time auditing unaccountable organizations that withhold or sugar-coat information, thereby creating additional regulatory costs—often levied back on those regulated. High employee turnover occurs when people feel a lack of trust from secretive management. As well, creditor relationships may become strained.

2. No rewards are offered for cost efficiency or seizing opportunities: Accountability extends to an employee's desire to ferret out excess cost and then minimize it. Some independent studies argue that the average employee in the United States wastes six weeks per year retrieving misplaced information from files. Americans as a whole waste nine million hours each day looking for lost items, amounting to a national loss of almost $150 million each day. Even though computers were expected to bring about a paperless society, we use approximately 50 percent more paper now than ten years ago, with 80 percent of all information still maintained on paper. Eighty percent of filed papers are never referenced again, and 50 percent of all filed materials are duplicates. Although use of electronic databases and storage is now increasing rapidly, the payback period for technology investment has been a long, slow process. In every survey taken over the past 20 years, managing paperwork falls into the top 10 time-wasting activities of managers. This has an enormous impact on corporate profitability and is a prime area for accountability to have a positive influence.

3. When positive behavior is not rewarded, complacency is almost always part of the culture: There is no incentive to take initiative or seek cost reductions by finding efficient ways of doing things. An opportunity to please a customer is not a priority if incentives do not exist. Organizations drift toward mediocrity.

4. No exposure of wrongdoing: Fear or complacency prevents employees from treating company assets with the same care and protection as their own. Ethics deteriorate. Trust deteriorates. Poor attitudes develop.

5. No linkage between vision and action: Companies waste more time and money implementing change because employees do not have a clear understanding of expectations, are measured on the wrong behaviour, or are rewarded on time and seniority instead of goal accomplishment.

6. Indecision, or decisions based on poor information: This results in lost opportunity or, in the case of poor intelligence, charging off in wrong directions.

7. Difficulty hiring the best people: The cost here is mediocrity, less than stellar performance, and competitive problems.

8. Lost reputation: The result of a declining brand over time is the public perception that the organization is not worthy of respect, and usually a stronger competitor grows in stature.

The interesting thing about accountability-pushed organizations is they can exist without their leaders knowing the real costs. How many customers were lost and what might they have spent had they actually bought goods or services from the organization? What is the cost of lost reputation? Maybe the company is not invited to bid on a lucrative contract, or maybe the brightest people do not apply to work there because to do so would harm their own personal brand. What are the chances that employees at each level will meet the expectations managers have of them? Then there is the time and money lost making wrong decisions with poor information. Good behavior goes unrewarded, while bad behavior is not exposed.

In accountability-drawn organizations, how employees are measured by superiors is extremely important. Expectations, clearly communicated at each level, are critical. If we do not know exactly what is expected of us, it is very difficult to accept responsibility to achieve it. And, it is difficult for leaders to hold us accountable. Without accepting responsibility, how can we be accountable?

Speaking out against wrong is only one component of accountability. Other components include assuming corporate goals as personal goals, driving excellence in superb stakeholder care, and ferreting out new, more efficient ways of carrying out procedures. Courage to make suggestions or offer valuable new ideas requires self-confidence, self-esteem, and a strong operating system.

Leaders must communicate responsibility and roles more clearly, how our role affects overall corporate goal achievement, and the impact of one department's success or failure over another: "If management measures our department's performance alone, why should we care about performance in other departments? There is no benefit to me sticking my neck out. I won't be rewarded. As a matter of fact, I will probably be criticized for sticking my nose in where it doesn't belong." If employees understand the importance of their contribution to vision achievement, they are more likely to care about corporate success. If visions are not clearly communicated in terms of the expectations of each employee, personal accountability will meet those expectations purely by accident. Relying on accidents is not a good strategy.

Once expectations are clearly communicated, there must be measurements of, and rewards for, personal accountability for it to have any chance of being maintained.

The sum of all employee accountability shapes the organization's accountability. Since the probability of any given organization having all employees with strong accountability is remote, corporate accountability will be a mixture of attitudes. Most management does not know how accountable its employees are to stakeholders. If you ask them if they are accountable, the usual answer is "Yes." However, further questioning will likely reveal only that rules, regulations and procedures are in place to provide guidelines for employees. Rarely is there accountability training to enrich corporate responsibility. And, rarely does management understand or act on the anatomy of accountability.

A Sense of What Influences Accountability

So, how does accountability evolve? What influences a person to be accountable? How is it reinforced, or not, throughout life?

We are born with a certain intelligence and predisposed genetics that affect us in different ways. Heredity becomes our starting point, the foundation to build a life on; no matter how weak or strong, it is the hand we are dealt. Whether we are smart, average or below average, nervous or brave, it's just the starting point. But this alone does not determine accountability, as a great deal of learned behavior follows. Intelligence, for example, doesn't determine whether or not we are accountable. Below average people in the right position, properly trained, may be more accountable than the brightest chief executive officer.

Consider a retail store cleaner. He is reliable, maintains high standards of cleanliness throughout the store, and is cheerful to customers. Some days he finishes cleaning early, and when he does, he helps the inventory clerk stock shelves, even though he is not expected to, and runs errands for the store manager in his spare time. He does everything expected of him with above average standards, and then helps others. Cleaning is his only responsibility. He does it extraordinarily well, then rises above his responsibilities to help others meet theirs. He could easily stick to his cleaning—that is what he is paid to do—but he knows that if the store is to do well, all jobs must be done well.

Now, consider a chief executive officer who minimizes information concerning a bad quarter to his board of directors, and then conceals looming layoffs to employees. He relies entirely on his direct reports to communicate corporate vision to the rest of the organization. He is intellectually brilliant and has an MBA.

It is clear who is more accountable. You may perceive that education or job description is a determining factor in who is accountable and who is not, but it isn't. Those who are accountable are those who treat the assets of the company as if they were their own.

A certain portion of personality is determined by genetics, but most of the credit for it belongs to the formative years. Our cleaner is a happy person who enjoys his job and the people around him. His personality is a strong, positive one. This asset enhances his ability to demonstrate strong accountability. Our chief executive officer, on the other hand, inherited his father's nervous insecurities and is somewhat paranoid about what people think of him. Consequently, his every communication and action focuses on placing himself in a better light. He puts his own interests ahead of the organization's. This fogs his ability to be personably accountable. What we inherit by way of intelligence, personality and health is our opening accountability balance sheet—composed of personality assets and liabilities that help or hinder the effective development of accountability.

If children are permitted to blame others for their actions, to be irresponsible without consequences, there is less chance they will be accountable as adults. If there are no personal accountability traits created and encouraged during the formative years, we enter adulthood "accountability handicapped." A strong mentor and work environment may possibly reverse this later, but with difficulty. On the other hand, children raised on trust, integrity and other strong values tend to be more open, less defensive and more self-confidant. They tend to act rather than wait to be told. They look for ways to better their environment rather than waste energy blaming others.

Institutions that influence us also play a role in shaping accountability. Corporations, governments or religious organizations may disappoint us with poor ethics, behavior or beliefs, contributing to our cynicism and perhaps weakening our standards of accountability: "Jim puts in the minimum amount of time on the job, why should I work any harder?" "Politicians can say one thing, and then do another

Leadership Gurus Speak Out!

and waste my tax dollars; why should I pay income tax?" "The church has taught me to treat others as I wanted to be treated, and then they abuse children and hide behind lawyers just like any other corporation." These sentiments can fog our lens of accountability and resulting conduct. If our lives are bombarded with examples of poor accountability from institutions we once held in esteem, over time our own accountability may deteriorate. Cynicism grows. We become more skeptical. We claim expenses of marginal validity on our income tax returns, justifying it by telling ourselves that the government taxes too much. Strong operating systems are less likely to permit influencing institutions to water down our values. We may disapprove of their actions but not use them to excuse unaccountability in ourselves. Weaker operating systems tend to use influencing institutions as props for cynical attitudes, excuses for less than enthusiastic behavior. Poor attitudes result in reducing our ability to be accountable.

Experienced mentors, successful in life, may positively affect accountability. However, subjects must be comfortable enough to accept mentoring, that is, not to take constructive criticism personally. They must be sufficiently self-aware to desire improvement. A strong mentor can bring you a country mile on the accountability scale. They raise confidence levels, depersonalize helpful criticism, and bring out our best qualities. The mentor must have strong interpersonal skills to motivate the subject, have the credibility of experience, and project an air of trust. Subjects of mentoring must trust, above all else, for without trust there will be no improvement.

Mentors can make up for certain aspects of poor formative years. Accountability-pushed people with lower confidence levels can be coached into better behavior with patience. But, they have to want to change.

Generational influences can produce periods of sustained impact and may also become forces affecting accountability. Children of the Depression grew up learning to be frugal; they were savers and recyclers and despised waste, because they had nothing during their formative years, their parents having had difficulty making financial ends meet. They worked hard for very little and were grateful for a job, no matter how menial. Baby boomers, on the other hand, grew up during the biggest period of prosperity in history; a generation of plenty hitting the job market during a period when the average number of years of post-secondary education increased and jobs were plentiful. People not only spent more money, they changed jobs more often. Spending was often careless; savings sometimes non-existent. Loyalty between employer and employee declined. More leisure time was demanded. All of that affected attitudes in the workplace; all had some immeasurable impact on the generation's desire to be accountable.

So now we have derived a sense of why people react differently to accountability and the challenges we face given different situations. The question becomes, how do we as employers create the most accountable team possible when everyone we hire arrives on our doorstep with an already formed personal operating system that guides their view of accountability? Add to that the fact that some see accountability as a minor consideration, others see it as essential.

So, What Should We Do?

In simplistic terms, we must create an environment that openly encourages accountability and makes it something all employees desire and strive to be recognized for. We actually build an accountability culture—one that links the corporate vision with expectations of employees, communicated at each level of the organization, clearly showing their impact on overall organizational success. This must be reinforced by a formal employee evaluation system composed of accountability goals, as well as financial and non-financial goals. As accountability goals are reached, the employee is praised and highly rated in the evaluation system, which in turn translates into rewards. This concept is one of linkage between corporate goals and individual goals, the achievement of which rewards both the company and the individual. Building this culture requires the company to:

- Develop and implement a training program for new hires that identifies good and improper behaviors through live and plausible case studies to show the desired way to behave;
- Mentor employees who need accountability improvement;
- Link employee goals with corporate goals at each level and build a formal evaluation and reward system around the linkage;
- Recognize outstanding accountable behavior publicly through town halls, emails, and one-on-one praise;

- Provide accountability, ethics and leadership training to link new responsibilities with the corporate vision each time an employee is promoted to a new level of responsibility;
- Celebrate whistle-blowers as heroes;
- Have a CEO who speaks of both success and failures, as well as lessons learned;
- Have a board of directors that admits to both good and bad decisions;
- Achieve excellence in stakeholder care—the overriding principle.

Building a Culture of Accountability

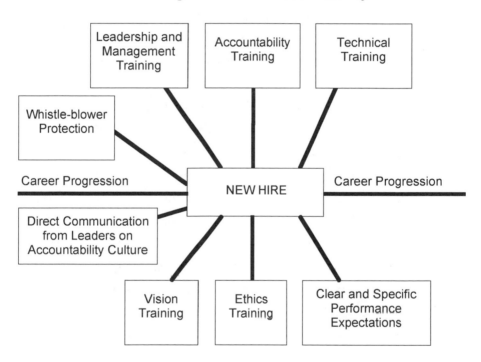

Imagine the potential impact of accountability training for new company hires. If taught the importance of honesty, trust and team playing, while giving whistle-blower protection and training in accountability, how much time would be saved by avoiding employee blame games? How much improvement would be realized through initiatives to grow sales as a team and cut costs, product times to market, rework, false project starts, and poor execution of action plans? How much more competitive would the company be? Add to this, new accountability training as each person is promoted to a new level so that as responsibility grows, so does accountability.

It would be ideal if we could test a new hire's propensity to be accountable. At the moment, this is socially unacceptable because it singles people out for profiling. However, it would make training programs more effective and focused by streaming potential employees into different levels. However, it *will* come, and even faster if there is another accountability disaster in the marketplace.

Vision training ensures that the corporate vision is broken into separate responsibilities for each level of employee and clearly explains the impact of successful or unsuccessful performance on other groups within the organization.

Direct communication from the chief executive officer and other leaders on the company's overall accountability performance should be frequent and meaningful to maintain a high level of awareness. Frequency, consistency and quality of communication lend credible support to the process.

Performance evaluations, based in part on achieving accountability goals, include financial and other rewards for growth in accountable behavior. So by the time employees reach the senior ranks, they are steeped in a culture of accountability.

A culture of accountability, by nature, concerns itself with outperforming competitors in stakeholder care, continuous improvement, learning from mistakes rather than assigning blame, aggressive sales, and profit growth. As such, accountable organizations will tend to attract more investment, more customers, and a higher quality of employee, incur less turnover, and enjoy a higher level of community respect than organizations that are not accountable. The next generation of business cannot afford to ignore creating such a culture. To ignore the anatomy of accountability and the creation of a successful culture will mean throwing away the next wave of business success.

Peter M. Cleveland

Peter M. Cleveland, BBA, FCA, CFE, CIRP (ret'd), is a strategic and business planning specialist who assists companies create and implement their strategic direction by linking visions to specific goals and actions over periods of three to five years. In doing so, Peter often assumes the role of part-time senior executive to advise management teams on leadership, planning—both strategic and operational—and defining the corporate culture necessary for success.

He is currently an executive-in-residence at the Telfer School of Management, at the University of Ottawa, as well as co-chairman of the Ottawa Hospital Foundation's capital campaign, and a member of the Board of Directors of CATA Alliance.

Peter is the author of *50 Steps to Business Success: Entrepreneurial Leadership in Manageable Bites*; *Corporate Ladders, Human Rungs*; and *Money, the Root of All Happiness*, as well as numerous business articles.

Business Name: Cleveland Leadership Group Inc.
Address: 5 Woodthrush Green, Ottawa, ON K1V 0A9
Telephone: 613-564-3868 or 613-371-0567
Email: clevelandleadershipgroup@rogers.com
Web Address: www.clevelandleadershipgroup.com

Leaders need to be optimists. Their vision is beyond the present.

Rudy Giuliani

Cy Wakeman

Cy Wakeman, Inc.

Leaders! Change Your Thinking to Change Your Life

Change…to make or become different. To replace with another. Change is the goal oftentimes seeming to be just outside our reach. The goal we often work towards but frequently cannot obtain. How many times have you set out to change your life or organization, only to feel that the attempt was short-lived or the desired change was unobtainable? You are not alone. According to John Kotter, an expert in change management, 75 percent of our efforts to change fail to produce the desired results. This means, conversely, we are successful only 25 percent of the time in our attempts to make a meaningful change in our lives. In general, we appear to be limited not only in our abilities to respond to change, but also in our abilities to initiate and sustain the changes we desire on a personal level.

Due to these seemingly dismal odds of success, we have become a cynical crew. In our companies, we end up settling for "profitable mediocrity" rather than striving for our "stretch goals" of inspiring and motivating employees, truly and completely satisfying customers, and being environmentally responsible. In our personal lives, we may accept those extra 20 pounds as the inevitability of middle age. We often resign ourselves to living with financial instability and living paycheck to paycheck. We then blame it on today's new economy. Even in our most personal relationships with others, we tend to settle for safety and routine rather than taking the risk and doing the work necessary to bring us pure joy and true intimacy.

We have adopted a settler's way of life,
rather than a thriver's way of life.
We settle for good when we desire and deserve great.

How have we ended up here? Have you settled for less in your life? Our failings are not due to a lack of knowledge, effort, focus, desire or even intent. Most of us approach lifestyle or organizational change with great effort, but not effective effort. We typically seek to change our circumstances rather than ourselves. We tend to attribute our lack of results to a variety of outside influences: limited resources, too little time, multiple demands, difficult circumstances, or other people's interferences. The reality is that our lack of results is really due to half-hearted attempts at changing our circumstances without first recreating our mindsets. Have you come to believe that the solution to your problems is at the mercy of circumstances? When faced with limited resources and/or limiting circumstances, we can obtain amazing results only by recreating our mindsets. When we recreate our mindsets and think in new ways, each new thought will eventually become our reality.

Exercise
Take a moment to entertain the following question:

If you *knew* you could not fail, what would you be creating in life?

_____

_____

_____

Did you answer—your ideal healthy body at its optimum weight and condition? Financial freedom? Healthy loving relationships? Great profitability and quality of life in your companies? Amazing results from your endeavors?

Leadership Gurus Speak Out!

Now consider your circumstances:

What is keeping you from your amazing results—from living the life you were meant to live?

_____

_____

_____

Do the challenges that you noted involve other people, places, things or conditions outside of your control? Are the issues not enough time? Not enough money? Lack of support from others? Or perhaps you wrote something about yourself, which is untrue, that you are somehow incapable or flawed. It is not external circumstances that have kept you from successfully making any changes so far. It is that a part of you doesn't believe that attaining your desires is possible.

**Our belief systems about ourselves and our circumstances,
whether positive or negative, heavily influence our mindsets.
Our past experiences, fears and disappointments often
trigger a series of negative self-statements, resulting
in a mindset that does not allow us to succeed.**

Recreating Your Mindset

Are you ready to recreate a mindset that can help you achieve results beyond your wildest dreams? The process is simple. It involves creating new thoughts and cultivating the virtues which already lie within you. Seem fluffy and unbelievable? I thought so too until I was faced with the opportunity to change my mindset and create amazing results for myself. I would like to share my story with you:

>> Three years ago I was in the prime of my life: happily married with four beautiful boys, running a successful consulting business, and actively involved in my community. Though truly grateful for my many blessings, a few things remained outside my reach. While achieving some great results and putting in a great amount of effort, my three most cherished values—health, family and financial freedom—were areas where I was

finding the least amount of success. It appeared I was attaining my goals, yet I weighed 260 pounds, spent very little time with my family, and continued to struggle to make ends meet. Why wasn't my hard work paying off? Why weren't my efforts creating the results I desired?

While sharing my frustrations with a girlfriend over coffee one afternoon, she challenged the ways I had been thinking about my goals. She observed that it was my tendency to place my focus on my efforts rather than on my belief system. She challenged me to start thinking about who I really wanted to be and to simply make choices as if I were already that person.

How could it be that simple? I opened myself up to the question, and the universe responded with tremendous learning. Great books, inspiring workshops and motivating people were put into my life. I allowed my thinking to be interrupted and it changed my life. **«**

Be It! I took my friend's suggestion to heart and began to be the person I wanted to be. In just six short years later, I now weigh 100 pounds less, have completed one marathon and am training for a second, am completely debt free—*and* I spend more time with family and friends. The changes seem to have come effortlessly. What caused my success? It came through believing that my goals were truly attainable—for whether I believed something was possible, or impossible, either way I was right.

The missing link to initiating and sustaining lasting lifestyle change is this: in order to change your life, you must first change your thinking and then devote your energies to the cultivation of virtues, rather than focusing on your results and external circumstances. This theory can be easily applied in the workplace as well. I have come to see amazing turnarounds in the companies for which I work when we place the focus on the people rather than the circumstances. If we can get the employees to believe differently, the results will follow.

Dynamic Approaches for Changing Your Life!

What follows are three key principles for transforming your life and/or the environment of the organization in which you work. They are:

1. Know that circumstances change when mindsets change;
2. Recognize that our most powerful limitations are self-imposed;
3. Incorporate the Be It! Do It! Have It! approach.

These are the principles to lasting lifestyle and organizational change. If you work to adopt these thoughts as your own, you will begin to experience results beyond your wildest dreams.

#1—Circumstances Change When Mindsets Change

Within each problem lies a disguised opportunity...but it is the art of unmasking the disguise that distinguishes between the two.

Jamie McDuff

We all have challenges in our lives. Recall the earlier exercise in which you identified the inner barriers that stand in the way of your ability to live your life fully. Did you notice that many of these issues are not new developments? Our challenges are typically persistent and recurring throughout our lives. It often seems as though we enter our lives carrying a "briefcase" containing a set of file folders. These file folders hold the themes of the challenges we face in our lives. The challenges and issues in these file folders manifest themselves over and over again in our physical reality, in the problems we have with our weight, our relationships, our finances, or even through a series of unfulfilling jobs. Life is a process of courageously opening the "briefcase" and embracing challenges as opportunities for profound learning.

Our typical approach to initiating change in our lives is to focus our efforts on creating different circumstances. We often act in ways that are self-defeating, rather than self-actualizing. This self-defeating process takes on a very common pattern. When we first become aware of a situation we would like to see changed, we typically respond with wishful thinking (e.g., the weight will drop off, we will win the lottery, next month will be better). We pretend that the challenge is temporary or we discount its full effect on our lives. Due to our disregard, the issue becomes a worse problem and its effect becomes more obvious. Since the issue will not subside on its own, our next approach is usually to jump into our "BMWs" (our bellyaching, moaning, and whining wagons). We collude with others who have similar "challenges," e.g., slow metabolisms, the economy, our bosses or the company leadership. By doing this, we agree that we are victims of our circumstances and come to believe that in order to accomplish any changes, we must first change our current circumstances—the people, places and things in our lives. When our attempts to change others and external conditions fail, we use these failings as "gas" in our "BMWs" and drive on to recreate this self-defeating cycle over and over again, each time expecting different results.

> **We seek quick answers rather than working to perfect our questions. We ask, 'Why does everything keep changing?' rather than, 'What do I need to do to respond to change more effectively?' We wonder, 'Why am I stuck with this state of affairs?' rather than 'What is my lesson to be received from these events?' We even begin to pray for our circumstances to change, for answers to become clear. Often our prayers go unanswered as God works instead to change us.**

Our life challenges are an exciting invitation to do something differently. Our response to these challenges, regardless of their nature, is what determines the depth and width of our lives. When faced with the many challenges posed to you in life, do not pray to change your circumstances, but rather to change the way you see your circumstances. By seeing things differently, you will be able to reframe your challenges and see them as opportunities to know yourself better. Life truly changes when you can find meaning in your suffering. At the minimum, your challenges offer you a practice ground for developing spiritual virtues such as courage, perseverance, integrity and wisdom. At the maximum, these challenges, when embraced and welcomed, give you the opportunity to know your greatest self first-hand. It is such a joy to find out that you are far more magnificent than you could have imagined!

Go back to the previous exercise and take a second look at the challenges you listed. Take a moment and reframe each one into the lifestyle change opportunities they represent. For example, by addressing head-on my excess weight, I had the opportunity to develop perseverance, courage, choice and commitment. These are the same qualities that, now developed, benefit me as I work to help others make lasting lifestyle changes.

Challenge	Opportunity
_____	_____
_____	_____
_____	_____
_____	_____

#2—Our Most Powerful Limitations Are Self-Imposed

The issue is not whether you have a significant problem to resolve but whether it is the same problem you had last year.

John Foster Dulles

After enough rounds of the self-defeating cycle described earlier, we develop a type of battle fatigue. We tire of trying to resolve the same issue in our lives year after year while experiencing little success. We delude ourselves into believing that we are putting forth whole-hearted efforts to change, when in fact our efforts are often half-hearted. We typically focus more on staying safe and comfortable while trying to change external factors first. We begin to attribute our lack of results to external factors outside our control rather than to our own choices. Finally, we come to believe that we no longer have the ability to impact our own outcomes. With enough setbacks, we come to live in a dangerous state of "learned helplessness," a psychological affliction affecting our belief system and our confidence.

If you have been struggling with an issue in your life with little success, you eventually will become accustomed to being at the mercy of your circumstances. You may even experience a sense of defeat before beginning new change efforts in your life or organization. Your current reality becomes clouded with past, self-defeating beliefs. What you lose sight of is the awareness that the disappointments you experience are an outcome of your own self-imposed limitations. In fact, we limit ourselves far more than our circumstances limit us! Let's look at the following two examples:

Example 1: Something happens so that an employee's behavior appears to be obstructive at this moment. You unwittingly expand this limitation exponentially by thinking that this person is always unsupportive. Once you have taken your belief to the point that this employee is always unsupportive, it becomes easy to jump to the conclusion that he/she is always difficult and you are, therefore, unable to ever bring new ideas to the table.

Example 2: You travel for work and you have found it difficult to find the time, place or energy to exercise. Since you may have missed a session or two, you come to believe that it is impossible to maintain a routine. You then expand this limitation to say that you are unable to exercise when you are on the road. You may even add the belief that without a strict regimen you won't see results anyway, and decide that exercise is not worth attempting, regardless of the situation.

It is our own additions to our limitations that keep us trapped in a state of learned helplessness. To move out of learned helplessness, it is vital to diligently challenge old patterns of thinking and behaving so that new possibilities and beliefs can be created. The process of moving out of learned helplessness is twofold. We need to first rigorously challenge our beliefs and then account for our individual contribution to our current state of affairs. In doing so, we can gain the freedom to make different choices as we go forward.

The only way to find out if the limits under which you have been living are real is to truly test them. If what you believe is limiting you is actually doing so, then this limiting factor will continue to exist when faced with ongoing testing. A great way to challenge any limitation is to choose to believe "I can" until proven otherwise. Unchallenged beliefs become powerful masters of our destiny. We must always pose the powerful question, "Is this belief really true?"

Let's practice this theory on the challenges you have already identified. For each item listed, design a mental or behavioral challenge. Ask yourself the following questions, carefully considering your answers:

- Is this really true?
- Do I know first-hand this is true?
- Am I making any assumptions?
- Could I be wrong?
- How do I know this?

- Do I truly need this in order to succeed?
- Is there a way to succeed in spite of these circumstances?

Make the commitment to get more information about any of the questions that you were unable to answer truthfully. Have a conversation, learn new skills, seek counsel of other women, choose to allow space for not knowing, and be confident that the answer is somewhere within. Seek to understand rather than to be understood.

Now that you are better aware of your true vs. self-imposed limitations, think of a time when you didn't get the results you desired. Write down as many details as you can recall regarding what happened and how you responded. Revisit your story; note the occasions on which you attributed your lack of results to external factors. Was your focus on what was done to you and who was to blame? Look closely and pick out all the assumptions you made, things you denied, choices you made, and items you ignored which led to your results. Rewrite your story, building in your own accountability. True accountability is simply having the ability to account for how you got to the place you are at today. Accountability is not about blaming others or blaming yourself. By accounting for the choices that led to your current results, you gain the ultimate freedom—the ability to respond differently. End this exercise by identifying choices that will better ensure your desired results. By doing so, you will begin living by choice rather than by default.

#3—Be it! Do it! Have It!

> You must be the change you wish to see in the world.
>
> Mahatma Ghandi

In the previous section, you worked to discover and challenge your beliefs in relation to your circumstances. Next, we will identify the role that our beliefs about ourselves and our potential plays in the outcomes we attain.

In our personal lives, we make New Year's resolutions or set goals for ourselves. When we set these goals, we give little thought or time to examining our ideal state of "being"—that person we truly want to be. We focus instead on logistical concerns and the resources that are needed in order to get there. Our typical process begins by only briefly identifying who we want to be. We then immediately begin to consider all the resources we will need to accomplish our goal. We then create a set of plans detailing all the actions we need to perform in order to get to our desired future state. This is a self-defeating process for it focuses on the circumstances of change rather than the mindset (Be It!). We find ourselves repeating the process year after year, expecting different outcomes. There is a flaw in the logic of the process, not in our ability to carry out the plan. Let's take a personal example to illustrate the problem with the process:

> » I wanted to be a runner from the time I was ten years old and I watched my first cross-country meet. I wanted everything that the women runners represented: strength, endurance, confidence, speed, muscles, health and beauty. I could hardly wait to come of age and join the track team.
>
> Finally, the first day of practice arrived and I ran a few laps at the request of my coach. At the end of practice, he excitedly shared his plan for my track future—he saw me as his lead contender in the shot-put throw. He pointed out that I was not built like a runner, but I could potentially have great success in the field events. He turned out to be right—I was successful in the field. I came to believe in that critical moment that I was not capable of being a runner. For the next 20 years, this disappointment would haunt me each time I caught a glimpse of a woman running.
>
> Every couple of years I would decide to give running another shot and would begin with the traditional planning methods. I thought first about all the items I would "have to have" in order to become a runner: running shoes, running suit, stopwatch, etc. Purchasing an item gave me the distinct feeling that I had accomplished a step toward my goal. Next would be to identify all the things I would need to be able to "do" in order to become a runner: weight training, doing laps, eating well, etc. My "having" and "doing" list grew longer over the years, and while I stayed on it, inevitably I would eventually fail again. After each failed attempt, I would confirm my coach's story about me. It became my story.

I came to believe that I wasn't cut out to be a runner. Instead of building a path to success, I had built a list of reasons, stories and potential excuses to fall back on in case I didn't get the results I wanted. The approach of focusing on "having" and "doing" rather than on "being" is what ultimately prevented me from becoming a runner. **«**

Life changes can occur in that moment when you decide who you really are and picture what it is you really desire. When you resolve to become the person you want to be, you need to first be that person. This concept became very clear to me one day as I gave a keynote presentation. With the audience, I shared my dream of becoming a runner. Afterwards, a woman from the audience waited for me. She was very excited to hear of my desire to become a runner, for she had become a runner late in life. She indicated that she would be thrilled to work with me in order that I, too, could know the joys of being a runner. While I was grateful for her offer, I began to share with her my reasons, stories and excuses as to why I couldn't take up running at that moment in my life. She pointed out that it wasn't about what I had to "have" or needed to "do" before becoming a runner, but rather about whether I believed I was capable of being a runner. "Decide that you are a runner and commit to a life of running," she advised. With much persuasion on her part, we set a time to run the next day.

With her continued challenging of my self-limiting beliefs, I went from being able to run three miles to completing the Chicago marathon—a 26.2-mile course—all in just 18 weeks! Over this time, I realized that the key to my success was in reversing the traditional method of planning for change, and focusing on "being" a runner rather than on feeding into my self-limiting beliefs. I acted like a great runner while growing into the part. Things became simple once I saw myself as a runner: simply run, eat well, stretch and rest, and get a great pair of running shoes and some comfy clothes (which I had previously classified as pajamas). Once I had publicly committed to being a runner and began introducing myself as a runner, dozens of people came forward to ensure my success. They provided many of the things that were previously on my "had to have" shopping list, such as great books and magazines, running gear and sound advice. This whole process taught me two things: how self-determining my beliefs really are and how powerful committing to a course of action can be. What took courage was not crossing the finish line—it was stepping up to the starting line.

True lifestyle or organizational change arises only when we reject traditional planning and goal-setting models. We traditionally focus on the necessary tasks, behavioral changes and resources that are needed before we can reach our goals. Reverse the order of your traditional planning process. Use the format "Be it! Do it! Have it!" to help. Begin by defining in great detail your desired state of being. Once you or your group can align around that vision and truly commit, you will be ready to do whatever it takes to achieve the goal. "Be" your vision, and the importance of having exactly the right resources and the best plan diminishes and the stage is set for amazing results.

Have the courage to step up and name yourself something great, challenge your beliefs, choose to live fully, and commit to a path that will head you in the direction of your dreams. You are worth it!

> *When you are facing in the right direction, all you need*
> *to do is keep on walking.*
>
> Buddhist Proverb

Cy Wakeman

Cy Wakeman speaks from experience! She has a solid reputation for achieving amazing results in spite of her clients' limited resources and challenging circumstances. Clients in a wide variety of industries have discovered her ideas to be key in successful planning and implementation of new programs and systems.

Cy works with organizations and individuals that want to thrive in difficult times by discovering new solutions to old problems. Her programs that create amazing results include:

- Succeeding in Spite of the Facts
- Succeeding in Spite of Differences
- Be It! Do It! Have It!
- Leadership Lessons of Lewis & Clark
- Management Development Institute

Cy's unique background combines four successful business start-ups with 22 years of working and consulting in a variety of arenas, including manufacturing, government, high-tech and health care. Cy holds a M.S. in Health Care Administration and has performed a variety of roles in the health care arena. In addition, she has personally led strategic planning efforts, created and implemented management development programs, provided executive coaching, and conducted business process re-engineering.

Business Name:	Cy Wakeman, Inc.
Address:	1525 Douglas Street
	Sioux City, IA 51105
Telephone:	712-202-0285
	866-493-4262
Email:	cywakeman@aol.com
Web Address:	www.cywakeman.com
Speaking Affiliations:	National Speakers' Association, Nebraska Chapter

Change your thinking, change your life!

Leadership is the capacity to translate vision into reality.

Warren G. Bennis

Sue Edwards

Development by Design

You've Gotta Flip It on Its Head!
Four Key Strategies for Leadership Success

» Lorna sits facing me in her tailored pantsuit, hands tightly clasped, her jaw firmly clenched and says, "I've finally been promoted to the executive team. All the others on the team are men. What tips can you give me to fit in? I've also been getting some feedback that I'm too angry-sounding and edgy with people, which is intimidating others. What can you do to help me fix this?" **«**

What career moments have you experienced that remind you of this scenario? Have you ever found yourself longing for a cookbook on how to fit in, or wished you could be granted a quick-fix solution to change how others see you? If so, you are not alone.

Now, step back from this and consider another perspective. Can you recall a time when you've been frustrated by the seemingly false behaviors of others at work? Can you relate to the feeling of wanting to take a colleague by the shoulders, look her straight in the eye and say, "Just be yourself!" Oddly enough, the behaviors that get in the way of people having a positive impact on others are often the *very behaviors* they've been trying hard to demonstrate. How ironic is that?

In my coaching with leaders, I find they frequently discover that their long-held beliefs about what makes leaders successful flies directly in the face of what happens in real life. They demonstrate leadership characteristics based on commonly held beliefs, such as:

- **Belief #1:** All leaders must communicate verbally with power and charisma.
- **Belief #2:** Leaders must convey a steely strength.
- **Belief #3:** Leaders must compromise themselves for the good of the organization.
- **Belief #4:** Previously gained skills are the foundation for success at the next level.

Down the road, they get the startling wake-up call that these purposeful behaviors have not resulted in the successes they had hoped for, after all. Frankly, they would do better to flip these beliefs on their head!

True leadership success and your greatest impact comes from the flip side of behaviors that you may have been socialized to exhibit as a strong leader. Your real power lies in awakening to the leader already inside you rather than layering on externally driven leadership qualities like a corporate cloak.

I invite you to consider how four leadership success strategies may apply to you. You've gotta…

1. Listen to be heard;
2. Be vulnerable to be strong;
3. Be selfish to serve;
4. Let go of what got you here.

Success Strategy #1—You've Gotta Listen to Be Heard

Seek first to understand, then to be understood.

Stephen R. Covey

Great leaders are known for articulating powerful visions and then galvanizing people towards this vision. For the rallying cry to echo throughout the organization, the leader's voice must be heard.

Leadership Gurus Speak Out!

Yet, when I work with leaders moving into new organizations, and using my Clearing the 90-Day Hurdle™ process, I point to research showing that the most critical behavior in the first 90 days is to "listen, observe, and ask questions." The new leader who rides in on a white charger with a predetermined vision and strategy can find the organization quickly turning its back. He or she has not yet earned the right to be heard about ways the company needs to profoundly change course. A receptive audience for a new vision is nurtured through a leader who demonstrates intentional listening, observation, and reflection prior to creating a vision. Yes, the critical step that comes first is listening.

» Mike is a charismatic leader and an exceptional presenter. He has a particular gift for inspiring a large room full of people. His speeches paint a picture of an exciting future. His stories are engaging and spoken with a confidence that conveys his opinions as THE truth.

This gift helped Mike to stand out as a leader early in his career. However, as Mike progressed through higher levels of leadership, his direct reports and peers began to express concerns. They grew tired of the storytelling and wanted more interactive, reciprocal discussion. Frankly, they started to see Mike as being so focused on what *he* had to say that they felt they weren't being heard.

Mike would describe his relationships with his direct reports by saying, "We have great conversations!" As his coach, I pointed out that, in fact, he likely was having a great conversation—with himself—in front of an audience of direct reports. (I call it "speechifying.") There was no room for Mike's direct reports to process, question, and give their own reactions and ideas.

I challenged Mike to consider, "What would it be like to set aside the speech and simply listen, ask questions, and explore ideas with one another?"

Over time, as Mike has learned to incorporate powerful listening into his conversations with others, his relationships have strengthened. The accountability displayed by his staff has soared. Most interesting of all is that others in the organization are now more eager to truly listen to, rather than simply applaud for Mike's speeches. «

Sue Edwards

This is how it works with *being heard*. It seems that it's not the person with the loudest voice that is heard but, rather, the leader who exhibits the most powerful listening.

Women in particular are often coached to "speak up" to ensure they are heard. The traditional advice to women in a male-dominated sector is to assert themselves like the men and to communicate in a strong, powerful voice. My response is…a resounding *maybe*!

For some women, demonstrating more assertiveness in a group—particularly a group of men—is a critical developmental step. There is also strong merit in training one's voice, learning about the use of breath and knowing how to speak from the diaphragm. This is all great advice.

At the same time, those of you who are proponents of a strengths-based leadership philosophy will likely relate to an alternative strategy. How about a flip? Rather than simply focusing on strong verbal assertions, what about the value of leveraging innate *listening* skills by:

- Listening intently to what's really being said;
- Being the bridge that helps people hear what each other is saying;
- Listening for the "elephants in the room"—those unspoken assumptions that stall effective communication.

These are the strengths that good listeners bring, and they apply equally to effective listeners of either gender. Some of you can readily "hear" the dynamics in a room. Once others identify you as someone who listens so attentively that you can even hear what's NOT being said…they will relish learning what you hear and invite your insight. Your listening strength is, ironically, your ticket to be heard.

> *Being right too soon is socially unacceptable.*
>
> Robert A. Heinlein,
> American science-fiction writer

Coaching Questions

- If you have a tendency to "give speeches," even in one-on-one conversations, when could you replace this with true reciprocal dialogue?

- If you are a strong listener, how could you leverage this power and ensure that your observations are made available to the group?
- If you are not a naturally strong listener, how might you develop this muscle?

Exercise

Here's a simple, yet revealing exercise to raise your awareness of the impact of "feeling heard."

- During the next two weeks, notice what happens when you don't feel heard. How does this impact YOUR ability to fully listen?
- Observe yourself in various situations—both at work and home.
- If you can, ask others what they notice about you at these times.

Success Strategy #2—You've Gotta Be Vulnerable to Be Strong

Water is fluid, soft, and yielding. But water will wear away rock, which is rigid and cannot yield. As a rule, whatever is fluid, soft, and yielding will overcome whatever is rigid and hard. This is another paradox: what is soft is strong.

Lao-Tzu (600 B.C.)

Think of times when you've felt vulnerable at work. Asking for help may have left you feeling vulnerable with the person you asked. Or, you may have experienced regret after admitting a weakness or disclosing a need for personal development to others. This is very natural in a society that teaches that vulnerability represents weakness. In fact, definitions of vulnerability refer to susceptibility to physical or emotional injury, criticism, or attack.

Yet, time and again, I've seen employees walk over hot coals for leaders who express vulnerability versus those who convey omnipotence. It is difficult to hook in at an emotional level with a leader who wears an armor of perfection. Much of my coaching work with both male and female executives involves supporting them in removing the Teflon® layer of self-protection that gets in the way of their ability to lead from a place of true power. They are inevitably seen to be stronger leaders as they mature in their willingness to demonstrate vulnerability.

Leaders who are able to deliver effectively stated requests for help are seen as resourceful and strong individuals. When they demonstrate the humility to ask for help, they earn the respect of others. In turn, the leader who asks for help is strengthened by the very support that is provided.

》 Kira recently made a shift in how she was interacting with her boss. When he asked her to prepare presentations, she assumed that she was expected to go away, develop the content, deliver it at the required meeting, and then wait for feedback from her boss. Her boss was highly regarded for the impact of his presentations and his openness in asking others for assistance. Kira, on the other hand, was well aware that presentations were not her strong suit. When she took a hard look at how this approach was working for her, Kira was able to see that she was not fully leveraging her boss's support. She could learn far more about creating presentations that have "oomph" by walking through a draft with her boss—focusing on the content plus her delivery—and obtaining feedback earlier in the process. So, she made the request for his upfront support.

The outcome? Her boss was delighted to coach Kira and was enthused about the opportunity to leverage his own strength and impart skills to her. By taking the time to work together preparing for a number of Kira's key presentations, she benefited from her boss's thought process. Kira's presentations now have punch! She delivers with the confidence of someone who has great material and is well-prepared. She now rarely needs corrective feedback after the fact. Equally important is that in the very act of asking for help, Kira has demonstrated to her boss that she is effectively leveraging resources around her. 《

Leaders also demonstrate strength in vulnerability through their response to receiving tough feedback. Many leaders have experienced 360-degree feedback assessments (surveys that provide feedback from the boss, peers, and direct reports). In observing the reactions to feedback for more than 100 leaders, it is clear to me that those who benefit most from a 360-degree process are those who disclose the results and build collaborative development plans in response. Recently,

Leadership Gurus Speak Out!

one of my coaching clients was told by her peers that it was extremely brave of her to reveal the themes in her feedback. They admired this disclosure and even asked how they could support her. Of course, the more support she receives, the stronger she becomes. The reinforcing cycle of strength through vulnerability continues to spiral upwards.

Coaching Questions

- How are your assumptions about vulnerability preventing you from building strong connections with others?
- If you had no concerns about being personally criticized, what might you disclose more openly?

Exercise

Consider an important goal that you are stuck on right now and can't seem to get any traction on.

- Think of someone you could ask for support to get you jump-started with respect to this goal. What specifically do you want to ask of them?
- How can you establish accountability to yourself to ask for help in achieving this goal?

Success Strategy #3—You've Gotta Be Selfish to Serve Others

[Spoken to a mother] *"How are you looking after your children's mother?"*

Dr. Phil (McGraw),

Television personality and psychologist

If we were to take Dr. Phil's philosophy about the importance of self-care as a way to serve others and apply it to you and your team, you might ask yourself questions such as: "How are you looking after your team's leader? (a.k.a. You)" and "Who is ensuring that your direct reports have a resilient leader who is clear-headed and who is modeling self-care?"

What may seem to be a very selfish approach to managing your role and your time is often the very approach that will best serve those around you over the long run. Consider that…

- In "selfishly" saying "No" to tasks that you are unable to complete within the required deadline, you are more honestly serving your customers.
- In "selfishly" asking your manager for exactly what you need from her, based on your own particular communication style, you create clarity and serve your manager and team well.
- In "selfishly" managing your work time so that you create space for your family life, you are serving your workplace by bringing a positive attitude and reduced resentment of your work.

When my coaching clients set clear parameters at work to achieve what they perceive to be their "selfish" *personal goals*, it has a profound positive impact on their productivity and satisfaction *at work*.

» Brian, a vice-president of operations whom I coach, has recently achieved fantastic improvements in his clarity and effectiveness at work. He started with one small personal commitment. Brian decided that every Thursday he would commit to taking his daughter to her after-school activity. He started structuring every Thursday so that he could successfully meet this commitment. This led to Brian finishing initiatives at work in time to leave the office. He was energized by *knowing* that he would be meeting a commitment to his family, instead of wasting energy worrying about whether he should stay at work or attend the after-school activity. For one day each week, the decision was already made. This became the parameter and work simply had to fit into the time allotted each Thursday.

The effect of this one small personal commitment rapidly began to spread. In no time, Brian could see that in meeting his commitment to his family and keeping his workday *defined* instead of open-ended, he became more efficient. His employer benefited, not just his family. His confidence strengthened as he began to redefine himself as someone who makes and keeps commitments to himself and others, instead of as someone who stretches to accommodate others' requests and compromises what is important to him. «

In our minds, we know that work always expands to fill the time allotted. Yet, as a society, we are uncomfortable setting limits. The bottom line is that it is often not until we "get selfish" and set limits that we become truly LIMITLESS in our impact.

One strategy to achieving greater productivity at work is blocking off certain times as "no meeting hours," or "email time," or "focused time for strategic projects." When it fits for their work, some people even schedule time to work at home or in another environment where there are no distractions or interruptions. Others schedule their fitness sessions into their calendar, to ensure that they respect these commitments to themselves. In "being selfish," they create a great return to those around them.

Coaching Questions

- What parameters do you need to set to ensure that you are meeting personal commitments, honoring your personal values, and remaining effective at work?
- If you were fully modeling the way you want your direct reports to look after themselves, what would you be doing differently?

Exercise

- What one small, "selfish" commitment can you make to yourself this week?
- What self-care habit or ritual will you establish regularly on an ongoing basis?
- How will you maintain accountability for this new habit?
- How will you celebrate when it becomes an established habit?

Success Strategy #4—You've Gotta Let Go of What Got You Here

If you only do what you know you can do, you never do very much.

Tom Krause, motivational speaker, teacher and coach

Sooner or later after a significant promotion, this challenge seems to hit all leaders between the eyes. Letting go of previously successful approaches is one of the most frequent coaching topics for my executive coaching clients. It's especially a challenge when the approaches that are no longer appropriate to rely on are the very behaviors that led to the promotion.

Why this sudden about-face? Why would certain behaviors be considered strengths one day and weaknesses the next? Are organizations this erratic?

Think of situations where you've been recognized for a particular strength—let's take "rolling up your sleeves and getting things done" as an example. For much of your career you may have been rewarded for showing initiative and accomplishing things yourself. Then suddenly as you are promoted to the director level, this strength doesn't seem to earn you the respect it once did. Your boss starts telling you to stand back and get things done through others instead. You are told to get your nose out of the day-to-day issues and address longer-term strategic concerns. You are encouraged to hold back your own answers and coach others to figure out their own best solutions instead.

» Valerie was recently promoted to Controller from the position of Manager, Strategic Alliances. In her previous role, she operated as an individual contributor. Her analyses of potential alliance opportunities required her to be very hands-on and focused on detailed information. She was recognized as being one of the strongest individuals in the company for knowing specific facts and being able to answer any question at all about the smallest piece of data.

In her new role, Valerie gained a team of managerial-level direct reports. In no time Valerie's team told her that she was micro-managing them. When she asked detailed questions about specific budget lines, they felt that Valerie didn't trust them. Her highest potential direct report resigned within one month, expressing that Valerie was too involved in the day-to-day details and required too much detailed information. Clearly, Valerie needed to let go of her detailed analytical strength and her desire to keep all of the details in her head. She needed to step up from individual contributor to a leader who "gets things done through others." Continuing to rely heavily on the skills she was recognized for in her previous job would sooner or later derail her at this new level. «

Interestingly enough, I've noticed that the challenge of making these shifts seems to be most difficult for people who have had the most previous success. The louder the applause, the more the individual wants to repeat the same behaviors. It can be frightening to move from a place of high achievement and strong recognition to a place of "not knowing" and uncertainty. It can be uncomfortable to move from expert mode to learner mode. It's very natural for this discomfort to result in resistance to pursuing new skills and a desire to continue relying on proven success strategies from past roles.

Accountability partners, such as your manager or a mentor, can be of great support in helping hold your feet to the flame and try out new behaviors. The services of a professionally trained leadership coach are particularly valuable to support you with these challenging skill transitions.

> *It is necessary to any originality to have the courage to be an amateur.*
>
> Wallace Stevens, poet

Coaching Questions

- What past skills or strengths are at risk of becoming (or may already be) liabilities for you at your current level in the organization?
- How can you shift your attention to the necessary new skills that are important for success in this role?

Exercise

- Consider the next significant developmental step ahead for you. Arrange a conversation with your manager, human resources, internal mentor, or external leadership coach to talk about what skill transitions are most important for success at the next level.
- How can you establish a plan for being deliberate about these skill transitions ahead?

So, Get Flipping!

Let's revisit Lorna, whom we met at the beginning of this chapter. Was she able to move from wanting a quick-fix approach to being coached? Did she learn to flip her leadership beliefs on their head?

» "Tell me about a leader you've worked with and truly admired," I asked Lorna in our coaching sessions. Her eyes softened and her shoulders relaxed. "Our previous CEO was revered by everyone. You knew where you stood with him and yet always felt cared for and as if you really mattered. He really looked after this company and he took time with people."

"Interesting," I smile. "Tell me again what you'd said about leaders who are warm never making it to the top in real organizations?" Lorna smiled too, "Point taken...but he could get away with it because he's a man." I held Lorna's gaze and asked, "What if your efforts to demonstrate such a tough exterior and operate in the way you perceive men to behave is actually getting in the way of you creating a positive impact? What if it was, in fact, undermining your strength? How might your 'edge' and 'anger' be a result of working so hard to portray an image that's not fully you?"

In a few short weeks after this "aha" moment, Lorna noticed the impact of "lightening up," listening more, and not charging in to make a point and demonstrate her expertise. In doing so, her peers were able to hear her advice and not see her as being on the attack or acting out of defensiveness. She started asking her colleagues for support in areas outside of her expertise and began sharing with them what she was trying to improve in her own leadership. She enrolled her boss in supporting her by providing feedback when he observed her trying out these new behaviors. Lorna started taking walks with a colleague at lunch and eating in the cafeteria instead of at her desk. She began trusting her direct reports to take on more ownership for initiatives themselves. This lightened her load, helped her feel better about their development, and caused others to see her operating at a much higher level. She was less uptight at work, worried less, and slept better. In working with all four strategies for leadership success, Lorna has begun to create a powerful platform from which to lead. She's become more herself and much more likeable to boot! **«**

To sum up, for me what's "hardest" about leadership has little to do with learning tips and tricks to fit in or to portray qualities that are not our own. The real work of discovering your leadership strength and optimizing your impact is figuring out how to stop trying so darn hard to be something that you're not and to lead from a more authentic place. I encourage you to challenge what you've long THOUGHT to be true about great leaders and listen instead to what you KNOW in your heart and in your gut to be true about who you are as your own best leader.

So I'm curious…what will you flip on its head to step into your full potential as leader?

> *Your time is limited, so don't waste it living someone else's life. Don't be trapped by dogma—which is living with the results of other people's thinking. Don't let the noise of other's opinions drown out your own inner voice. And most important, have the courage to follow your heart and intuition. They somehow already know what you truly want to become. Everything else is secondary.*
>
> Steve Jobs, co-founder of Apple

Sue Edwards

Sue Edwards brings a powerful blend of passion and professionalism to her coaching with executives and leadership teams and is an international conference speaker. She founded Development by Design in 1996 and she works globally with clients in various industries, including technology, manufacturing, consumer-packaged goods, as well as universities. She specializes in working with successful leaders transitioning into a new organization or upward into significantly more challenging levels of leadership. Sue previously held senior HR roles with Campbell Soup, Bayer, and Imperial Oil.

She is a graduate of Corporate Coach U and is an accredited coach at the ACC level with the International Coach Federation. Sue is an Industrial Psychology graduate from the University of Waterloo, with MBA courses from Dalhousie. She has achieved her Certified Human Resources Professional (CHRP) designation. Sue is qualified to administer MBTI®, Thomas International (DISC) Personal Profile™, and Benchmarks®.

Sue is the author of *Congratulations, You're Hired! A Coach's Guide to Ensuring a Successful Transition*. She is developing a workbook entitled, "Wow Them in Your New Job! (and Reduce Your Overwhelm)...It's Easier Than You'd Expect." She has been interviewed on CTV's "Canada AM" and profiled in the *National Post*. She writes regular columns on leadership issues.

Business Name:	Development by Design
Address:	19 Appaloosa Trail, Carlisle, ON L0R 1H3
Telephone:	905-690-0456
Email:	sue@development-by-design.com
Web Addresses:	www.development-by-design.com and
	www.clearingthe90dayhurdle.com
Professional Affiliations:	Human Resources Professional Association of Ontario;
	International Coach Federation; CoachesCanada.com;
	Company of Women; Career Professionals of Canada

Favorite Provocative Question:
If everything was possible and you had all the courage in the world, what is the bravest thing you could do?

Kathy Glover Scott

Alternative Truths Speaking and Consulting

Mastery and the Future of Leadership

The next time you walk into a major bookstore, notice the tables when you first enter the building. You will see the latest bestsellers, magazines touting the latest Hollywood scandal, and also prominently displayed will be books on spirituality and the soul, meditation, alternative health, eastern philosophies, and shifting consciousness. We have entered a new age, where the average person knows that there is more to life than simply living. People are no longer simply searching for meaning in their life; they are living life in a meaningful way and knowing that there is a higher purpose in all that they do.

This is no longer a way of life for a few. If the big bookstores are prominently displaying tables and shelves of spirituality, health and self-help books, you know that these are big business. And this movement of ideals and values for living is not going away—it is a powerful way of living that brings greater meaning to people's lives.

Know that this change is here to stay and will continue to evolve. People are in a transitory period, incorporating a new set of beliefs about themselves and their work.

In my work as a coach for leaders, it is clear that this shift impacts how they lead. Also, many leaders are incorporating these new values for themselves—and integrating them into the workplace.

This shift in consciousness and expectation for a genuinely fulfilling work experience is happening for leaders as well. Many leaders are experiencing an inner angst as their awareness grows that their old approaches to motivation, communication, problem solving and self-care no longer fit for themselves or their employees.

So where does this take us? Increasingly, employees want a genuine work experience that will align with and reflect their own personal inner evolution. At the same time, leaders are increasingly experiencing their own personal angst in their role as leader searching for fulfillment. They are being nudged by the needs and expectations of their employees to evolve both personally and to embrace a new style of leadership.

Leaders are being lead to shift how they lead.

It is as though many leaders are experiencing a hand in the middle of their back, gently nudging them forward to lead in a new way. With this comes the experience of an inner conflict for many, and may appear as stress, disillusionment over their role, lack of motivation, or vacillating between old controlling leadership approaches and new empowering ones.

It would be great to be able to hand you a document that outlines how to be an evolved leader. Unfortunately, that is not possible, as the template for this new style has not been written yet. It is still in its infancy. Changing markets and work expectations are impacting how we need to lead. Yet what is moving a leader forward more quickly, is the evolving employee. With employees desiring more genuine connection and meaning at work, leaders are called upon to evolve as well and shift how they lead. Knowing the tenants of masterful leadership provides the leader with the foundation to move forward and be in charge of this change.

Releasing Fear in Leadership

Until now, one of the primary driving forces for leaders has been fear. And the reason comes from the top—our models for organizational structure and how to do business developed in a time where "survival of the fittest" was their call to arms. Yet, in this global age, we are learning new approaches that are getting proven results. We've learned that successful selling can now be "attraction based." In international markets, we are learning that we are further ahead through collaboration and respecting diversity. And with instant access to information for everyone, leaders can no longer corner the knowledge market. All and all, using fear as the primary tool in your organizational and success tool kit no longer works.

Fear is a very primal force that feeds on relationships and structures based on taking energy from others and using it to feel more powerful in yourself. And fear is a hungry taskmaster—when it goes unquestioned and unchallenged in order to be satiated it will feed on everyone and anyone. In leadership, a fear-based approach is demonstrated through the belief that if you do not control others, you will be powerless. Ego is that part of the self that holds these beliefs and reacts from them in dealing with others.

The remedy for fear-based leadership is one based on mastery. The energy of mastery is a much higher force, flowing from the best of what a leader has to offer. Mastery is a force expressed from the core belief that a leader has about themselves in their role. It is a force and a frequency of energy that flows from the core of a leader, flowing through them and permeating those they influence and all they do. Being masterful is the result. That as a leader, you've reached a place of oneness and above average competency in your role. You no longer simply have a role, you have a presence.

Think of it this way: fear has a survival of the fittest mentality and belief system. It is reactive in nature and, being this way, it rarely allows a leader to see the "bigger picture" or bring new, stronger values into the workplace culture. Sure, the fear-based leader can and will try to lead in new and innovative ways—usually based verbatim on the latest leadership course they've taken—but change never seems to stick. A leader who realizes that fear and ego have no place in successful leadership, is a powerful catalyst in the workplace. A masterful leader is able to pull strengths, fortitude, creativity and achievement out of people who could never reach those levels on their own. And a masterful leader is a visionary who refuses to fear the unknown.

Leading with mastery rather than fear is a commitment to a high level of integrity, vision, strategy, and energy. And a masterful leader accepts living and working in a way that maintains this level and supports its ongoing evolution and expansion.

Exercise in Mastery

One of the most powerful ways to instill new beliefs and patterns of behavior in work and life roles is by aligning with a mentor. Those leaders who are ready to lead through mastery rather than fear often find it useful to bring this role into their evolving life. (Once you choose mastery in leadership, it permeates your entire life for the better.)

Great masters have always studied other great masters who passed before them to understand the energy and laws of mastery. For this exercise, select a great master who has passed before you and study their existence, influence, achievements, presence and energy. While researching his or her life, you may want to keep the following questions in mind:

- When and where did they/do they live?
- What are their familial, cultural and social influences?
- What are they passionate about?
- What special qualities do they have or emulate?
- How are they visionary and how are they challenged?
- How are they chosen?
- What motivates them?
- How are they personally tested in life?
- What strengths do they have and how did these carry them?
- What were their "weaknesses" and how did they overcome them?
- What kept their faith strong?

Though they may have lived in a different place and time, look for the parallels in their life with your own learning and growth process. You'll use these in the future to keep you grounded and focused as you strive be more fully a mastery-based leader. Making some notes as you go through this process is helpful.

The Elemental Foundation for Mastery

**A masterful leader engages in the process of personal
and professional evolution in their role. And they fully surrender
to who they are meant to be at this point in time. They
become self-actualized through their role as leader.**

Mastery is a force expressed from inner beliefs that a leader has about themselves and those they lead in their role. This force is a frequency of energy that flows through and from a leader. It permeates those they influence and all they do. One of the most powerful inner beliefs that a masterful leader holds is knowing that each person has their own unique brilliance. And that their role is to excavate and encourage the nugget of brilliance in all those they lead.

So, therefore, being a masterful leader is not solely about learning new skills and implementing them. It is about having a solid core of self in your role, knowing how to build and recharge this core, and allowing all of your direction and wisdom to flow from this. The following are some of the key elemental beliefs of masterful leaders:

Being a visionary in action: A masterful leader sees the bigger picture. It is almost as though you work and lead on several levels at the same time, holding the vision and needs of the organization while being able to translate it so that it is understood by the team and the individual—and sometimes even the client. As the leader knows that each person has their own unique brilliance, how they communicate the bigger picture is automatically charged with positive energy and each person comprehends the importance of their role in it.

Knowing there is always more than meets the eye: On a fundamental level, a leader knows that there is always more to issues, human dynamics, problem solving, and their role than is immediately perceivable. Being a masterful leader takes this further—knowing and believing that there is also a "higher purpose" to the group they lead and how they come together, interact and get the job done at this particular point in time. As a masterful leader, you hold this belief for the team which, in turn, provides a framework for problem solving and success at the highest levels possible. With this, you strive to fully let go of the belief that you can motivate others. Your role is to be the catalyst; to push the buttons that lead a person to release their own energy, skills and motivation from within themselves.

As leader you are living your "soul purpose": As a visionary coach, people come to me asking for help in uncovering their soul purpose. Often a person learns, through our work, that they are living out their purpose in the here and now. A masterful leader knows that your role is not a job or a position—it is part of your purpose in being here—and that those you influence have not been put in your path by chance. You know that each challenge is a chance for growth, that each conflict provides the opportunity for new insights and self-awareness and that each success belongs to those whom you lead. Your satisfaction comes through your experience as a catalyst and a force that allows the whole to be greater than one small part. And that you are leading from your soul and influenced by forces unseen.

As a leader, you help others to live their purpose: Whenever a team comes together, it is not by accident. Unseen forces, based on essential life lessons, bring this group together with you. Knowing this actually reduces stress for a leader. You no longer need to control or find all the solutions required. You become comfortable in knowing that leadership is about co-creation in a focused, intentional way. Know that each person you lead teaches you as much—or more—than you teach them as long as you are open to learning. This is your payoff. Which leads to our next point…

Masterful leaders are students of power: As a planet and a people, we are rapidly learning that our current understanding and operative use of power is archaic, does not promote effectiveness in organizations, and in many ways is destroying us.

The notion that power is "the controlling of others" is a very low-level form of leadership. Rather, a masterful leader knows that power flows from their own core of strength. The people that you lead respond to this strength, rather than react to the fear that is the energy of a "controlling" leader.

This does not mean that as a masterful leader, you are spineless. Rather, you become adept at identifying energy and focus being wasted. You become more comfortable with whistle-blowing when required, and do it with non-attachment. This means that you are clear as a bell—not personalizing the issue—and the recipient has a greater chance of experiencing your message this way.

As a masterful leader, you teach power without aggression to others. You can speak openly with staff about the strategic use of their own inner power and more effectively choosing to use their energy. People are really opening up to the power of thought. As a leader you master this yourself, so you can teach others to be observers of their own thoughts and to know that their body believes whatever their brain tells them.

Masterful leaders park their ego at the door: Masterful leaders are not afraid to let go of ego—or rather "toxic ego." Ego is the part of self that holds the core of who we are. A person with a toxic ego is one who is fear-based in his or her life, and as a result works to dominate and control others to feel in control and safe in the world.

As mentioned previously, the masterful leader no longer has the need to control those around them. They do not lead from a toxic ego, but rather a place of confidence. They choose to approach their staff, work and life from the proactive, responsive position rather than the fear-based, reactive approach. And even when stress is high, they are self-aware, know what triggers them, and learn to tame the fear-based ego.

The Alchemy of Mastery

The ancient art of alchemy is the process by which raw materials—usually lead—can be transmuted into gold. Mastery leadership comes through your openness and receptivity to listening and responding to the higher vision that you have for your work. Haven't you had the inkling that there is something more? There is!

At some point with any great growth or change, arises inner conflict and uncertainty. This can happen during the shift from leadership to mastery leadership. In this process, they do not deny the challenge in growth, but rather develop a deepening self-awareness and know that this is indicative of new insights, personal growth, and greater strength in their role. Basically, there will be times when frustrations arise, solutions are elusive and you seem directionless, while others are asking for your guidance. It is human nature to fight these times and isolate while "running around" trying to find a solution. Surrender to these times and ask for help—masters know that doing this is not a sign of weakness.

Think of yourself as being immersed in the energies of mastery. It is about owning your power and moving through life with the consciousness of mastery—a consciousness that will flow to all you meet, in the decisions and goals you make, through your daily work, and when activating the law of attraction.

You are evolving as a leader and being aligned with the energies of mastery. Choose to move forward as a masterful leader and revel in the rebirth you'll experience. This is about owning your power and moving through life with the consciousness of mastery—a consciousness that will flow to all you meet, in the decisions and goals you make, through your daily work and, of course, how you lead.

> To lead people, walk beside them...
> As for the best leaders, the people do not notice their existence.
> The next best, the people honor and praise.
> The next, the people fear;
> and the next, the people hate...
> When the best leader's work is done the people say,
> "We did it ourselves!"
>
> Lao-tzu

Kathy Glover Scott

Kathy Glover Scott, M.S.W., is the Mastery Guru. As a keynote speaker and facilitator, she weaves together best business practices with advanced energy work to help attain powerful results. As an executive and business coach, Kathy teaches mastery and how to live optimally each day. She is in demand as a cutting-edge keynote speaker and leader in innovative energy practices.

Kathy is one of only three people in North America accepted to teach Reiki to the 21st degree, as well as other advanced energy-based courses. Visit her website for speaking topics, online courses and upcoming programs in your area. Kathy is currently working on two writing projects focusing on mastery and shifting consciousness.

Books and CDs by Kathy Glover Scott:

- The Successful Woman
- Esteem! A Powerful Guide to Living the Life You Deserve!
- The Craft of Writing for Speakers (CD)

Experts Who Speak Books (co-publisher):

- Expert Women Who Speak...Speak Out! Volumes 1–6
- Sales Gurus Speak Out
- Awakening the Workplace, Volumes 1 and 2
- Leadership Gurus Speak Out

Business Name:	Alternative Truths Speaking and Consulting
	Experts Who Speak Books
Address:	Kanata (Ottawa), ON
Telephone:	613-271-8636
Email:	Kathy@KathyGloverScott.com
Web Address:	www.KathyGloverScott.com
Professional Affiliations:	International Federation of Professional Speakers; Canadian Association of Professional Speakers (Ottawa Chapter); Canadian Association of Professional Social Workers

Adele Alfano

Canada's Diamond Coach **Adele Alfano** is renowned as an expert in personal effectiveness and excellence, and change management. She has earned the reputation of being a "mining" expert in professional potential and personal empowerment. Nominated for Canada's 100 Most Powerful Women, Adele has been acclaimed for her energetic and content-rich keynotes and informative seminars. She has been described as a skillful and entertaining presenter who combines charm, wit, heart and passion.

As an award-winning professional and inspirational speaker since 1998, Adele has been a sought-after opening and closing conference keynoter, luncheon speaker, employee/volunteer recognition awards speaker, and seminar leader. Renowned for her proven techniques, she is privileged to have an extensive client list that includes large national associations, leading corporations, government, school boards, and the health care industry. Adele consistently receives rave reviews and standing ovations from audience members who find her presentations valuable, touching and informative.

Canada's Diamond Coach is the co-author, co-editor/ publisher of the *first ever* series of collaborative books by experts and speakers, entitled Experts Who Speak Books— www.expertswhospeakbooks.com.

Business Name:	Diamond Within Resources: Speaking and Consulting
Address:	P.O. Box 60511, Mountain Plaza Postal Outlet
	Hamilton ON L9C 7N7
Telephone:	905-578-6687
E-mail:	adele@diamondwithin.com
Web Address:	www.diamondwithin.com
	www.kissmytiara.ca
Professional Affiliations:	International Federation of Professional Speakers; Professional Member of the Canadian Association of Professional Speakers

Notes

Notes

Notes

Experts Who Speak Books

With this tenth volume in the **Experts Who Speak** book series, we are firmly established as an influential forum to globally promote professional speakers and trainers and provide them with the opportunity to be best-selling authors. If you are in the public eye and speaking, training or coaching is your field of endeavor, you may be interested in joining us. Our upcoming titles include:

- Expert Women Who Speak…Speak Out, Volume 7
- Awakening the Workplace, Volume 3

• • •

**Follow your dreams with intention and
passion and let the amazing journey unfold.**

• • •

*Kathy Glover Scott and Adele Alfano,
Publishers of Experts Who Speak Books*

For more information on upcoming volumes,
or how to be a contributor, please contact either:

**Adele Alfano www.diamondwithin.com
or
Kathy Glover Scott www.kathygloverscott.com**

Visit our websites:

**www.expertswhospeakbooks.com
www.leadershipgurusspeakout.com
www.expertwomenspeakout.com
www.salesgurusspeakout.com
www.awakeningtheworkplace.com**

Thanks to Creative Bound International Inc.
for assisting us in making this best-selling series a reality.
www.creativebound.com